Two to One

FOREWORD
by Chairman Steve Hamer

Two successive promotions, who would have believed that two years ago on that fateful last day of the season?

Add the extra ingredient of the sale of the Club to the Al Qadi family midway through last season, people can't say things have been uneventful at Bristol Rovers FC over that period!

After taking some time to acclimatise at the start of 2015/2016 season the team soon began to find its feet and although there was a major disappointment in losing at home to Chesham United in the FA Cup, steady progress was made after that set back.

On February 19th the Club appeared to be blessed with a lucky charm, new owners! From that day the team's form can only described as inspired, two defeats, two draws, and twelve victories culminating in possibly one of the most exciting final days of the season that the Club has ever been involved in.

The name Lee Brown will be indelibly etched into the memories of every true Rovers' fan's mind for rest of their lives.

Enjoy this publication, it's hopefully the first of many to come over the next few seasons.

STEVE HAMER
CHAIRMAN

Two to One

FOREWORD
by Manager Darrell Clarke

Two years ago this football club was relegated out of The Football League and it really was a devastating experience for everyone connected with Bristol Rovers.

The road to redemption, if I'm honest, began back then and after only one season of playing non-league football we were promoted back to League Two, via the play offs, last summer.

To gain a second successive promotion, therefore, is an unbelievable feeling and to do it in almost the final minute of the final game of the season was incredible.

I am so proud of all my staff, my players, and all of the club's supporters because to win back to back promotions is a credit to each and every one of the players and everyone who works so hard behind the scenes, from my own management team to those who work in in the club's offices.

I know I keep saying it, but this is a special club and to see the joy on people's faces after we clinched promotion was a magical moment.

We left it very late to clinch the winning goal and then had to wait a few minutes to see how Accrington had fared in their match against Stevenage. A late goal for them would have meant us contesting the play offs again, so when news of their goalless draw filtered through we knew we were up.

In all honesty I thought we deserved a little bit of luck and, while it's natural to feel for Accrington, it was an amazing moment for our club.

This squad has its share of characters; every player is strong, mentally, and it's a very close knit group and they deserve all the success they have achieved.

Last summer I said I wanted to see us challenge for a top seven place. I really don't see any point in aiming for a mid-table finish. We need to keep improving the club and to do that you have to be highly ambitious.

At the start of the season I told the players that if they didn't prove themselves to be a top seven team then they would be moving on. I'm always open and honest with them, and they certainly showed everyone just how good they are.

We finished the season on 85 points, lost just one of our last 14 games, ended the campaign with a ninth consecutive home win, and recorded a record equalling 11 away wins, which is why this group of players deserve all the plaudits that come their way.

It feels as though we have brought this club back together and that we are moving in the right direction and this record of a truly remarkable season is one for all Gasheads to cherish and to look back on with pride.

However, we need to build on what we have achieved in the last two years, both on and off the pitch, and we will be striving for success again when the 2016/17 campaign begins.

DARRELL CLARKE

Two to One

PREFACE
by Keith Brookman

On 3rd May 2014 Bristol Rovers ended a 94 year stay in the Football League when they were relegated on the final day of the season and faced up to the prospect of playing non-league football in what was then known as The Vanarama Conference.

Promotion back to The Football League was achieved via the play offs when Grimsby Town were despatched, in a dramatic penalty shootout, at Wembley on 17th May 2015.

The story of that one season in the non-league game was charted in last year's publication 'The Long Road Back' and, if I'm being absolutely honest, I wasn't convinced, until the last couple of months of the 2015/16 season, I would be writing a follow up to that particular book!

At the beginning of the campaign, there was a sense of pride around the club again. The one season in The Conference had been a new experience, but it wasn't league football and it was just good to be back.

Supporters seemed to feel the same and would, it appeared, be happy not to repeat the experience, not to say trauma,

of dropping out of the league again in a hurry. Consolidation, it seemed, would be fine!

The manager and his squad had other ideas and Darrell Clarke made no secret of the fact that he was targeting a top seven finish for his side. Given that some members of his squad had never before played league football, it seemed a tall order and the start of the season left them needing to add more consistency to their game if they were to fulfil their manager's ambitions.

An opening day defeat was followed by three consecutive wins, four losses in the next five games and then a run of four wins on the bounce. The biggest problem, though, was a lack of home wins; up until the beginning of December Clarke's side experienced no fewer than eight defeats at The Memorial Stadium.

However all bad runs, just like the good ones, come to an end and from the 3-0 win against Wycombe Wanderers until the end of the season only one more point was dropped, in a 1-1 draw against Plymouth Argyle in January. That run took in an impressive 14 games and, indeed, early December appears to have been the

turning point in the campaign and proved to be the stepping stone to success.

Away form was never a problem and Clarke's side equalled a club record of 11 wins on the road and as the campaign progressed they developed the look of a side that were always going to be difficult to beat.

As well as being a very talented group of players, there was a unity about the group; no one was excluded, there were no dressing room cliques and everyone got on, both on and off the pitch. Team spirit is often mentioned as a vital ingredient of any successful side and this group had it in abundance.

Credit for that goes to the manager and his backroom staff. The squad, developed in non-league football, improved again in League 2 and now look forward to the challenges posed by League 1 following the way that promotion was clinched on a dramatic final day of the season.

I hope you will all enjoy this written and photographic record of an amazing, and historic, season when Bristol Rovers achieved back to back promotions for the first time in the club's long history.

1 Jamie Lucas scores his second goal at Salisbury

2 Alfie Kilgour wins a header at Sutton

3 Billy Bodin on his way to a hat trick at Cirencester

4 Nathan Blissett in action at Mangotsfield

5 Chris Lines is challenged by Arsenal's Stephy Mavididi

6 Stuart Sinclair gets away from Reading's Anton Ferdinand

7 Tom Lockyer scores at Cheltenham

8 Daniel Leadbitter keeps a close eye on West Brom's former Rovers striker Rickie Lambert

■ ■ ■ Pre-Season Friendlies 2015 ■ ■ ■

Rovers played a total of eight first team pre-season games as they prepared for the 2015/16 campaign.

The highlight of the summer schedule was the testimonial match for Phil Kite on 31st July when Rovers entertained West Bromwich Albion.

The Baggies, managed by Kite's friend and former Rovers player Tony Pulis, signed former Rovers striker Rickie Lambert on the day of the game and he scored his first goals for his new club against The Gas on a memorable evening.

Saturday 11th July 2015
Salisbury FC 1   Bristol Rovers 4
Attendance: 1,068

Goalscorers: *Lucas (12 & 57), Blissett (53 & 90)*
Rovers: *Steve Mildenhall, Tyler Lyttle, Tom Lockyer (Alfie Kilgour, 69), Mark McChrystal, Danny Greenslade, Cristian Montano (Jay Malpas, 69), Stuart Sinclair (Dominic Thomas, 59), Jake Gosling (Ryan Broom, 69), Billy Bodin, Nathan Blissett, Jamie Lucas*

Sunday 12th July 2015
Sutton United 1   Bristol Rovers 2
Attendance: 658

Goalscorers: *Lines (15), Broom (80)*
Rovers: *Kieran Preston, Daniel Leadbitter, James Clarke (Alfie Kilgour, 66), Tom Parkes, Lee Brown, Jennison Myrie-Williams, Chris Lines (Dominic Thomas) Ollie Clarke, Toby Ajala, Ellis Harrison (Jay Malpas, 51), Matty Taylor (Ryan Broom, 46)*

Tuesday 14th July 2015
Cirencester Town 0   Bristol Rovers 7

Goalscorers: *Bodin (7, 16, 41), Lucas (pens, 33 & 81, 59), Broom (61)*
Bristol Rovers: *Steve Mildenhall, Tyler Lyttle, Tom Lockyer (Alfie Kilgour, 46), Mark McChrystal, Danny Greenslade, Ryan Broom, Stuart Sinclair (Jay Malpas, 60), Lee Mansell (Jake Slocombe, 60), Jake Gosling, Jamie Lucas, Billy Bodin*

Wednesday 15th July 2015
Mangotsfield United 0
Bristol Rovers 2

Goalscorer: *Blissett (31 & 60)*
Rovers: *Kieran Preston, James Clarke (Jake Slocombe, 70), Alfie Kilgour, Tom Parkes, Daniel Leadbitter, Ollie Clarke (Jay Malpas, 70), Chris Lines, Toby Ajala, Lee Brown, Ellis Harrison, Nathan Blissett*

Saturday 18th July 2015
Rovers 0   Arsenal XI 1
Attendance: 2,093

Bristol Rovers: *Steve Mildenhall, Daniel Leadbitter, James Clarke, Tom Parkes, Danny Greenslade (Jay Malpas, 76), Stuart Sinclair (Cristian Montano, 60), Chris Lines, Lee Mansell (Ollie Clarke, 46), Jake Gosling, Ellis Harrison (Matty Taylor, 46), Billy Bodin (Jermaine Easter, 60)*
Substitutes: Nathan Blissett, Jamie Lucas

Tuesday 21st July 2015
Bristol Rovers 0   Reading 2
Attendance: 1,880

Rovers: *Steve Mildenhall, Daniel Leadbitter (Tyler Lyttle, 46), James Clarke (Alfie Kilgour, 75), Tom Parkes, Lee Brown (Danny Greenslade, 46), Stuart Sinclair (Jay Malpas, 63), Ollie Clarke, Chris Lines (Jake Gosling, 46), Cristian Montano (Billy Bodin, 56), Matty Taylor (Nathan Blissett, 63), Jermaine Easter (Ellis Harrison, 46)*
Substitutes: Jamie Lucas, Kieran Preston

Saturday 25th July 2015
Cheltenham Town 2
Bristol Rovers 1

Goalscorer: *Lockyer*
Rovers: *Steve Mildenhall, Tom Lockyer, James Clarke, Tom Parkes, Danny Greenslade (Daniel Leadbitter, 46), Jake Gosling, Chris Lines, Ollie Clarke (Billy Bodin, 65), Cristian Montano (Stuart Sinclair, 46), Nathan Blissett (Matty Taylor, 46), Ellis Harrison*

Friday 31st July 2015
Bristol Rovers 0
West Bromwich Albion 4
Attendance: 4,086

Rovers: *Steve Mildenhall, Daniel Leadbitter, James C;arke, Tom Parkes, Tom Lockyer, Jake Gosling (Ollie Clarke, 62), Chris Lines, Stuart Sinclair, Billy Bodin (Cristian Montano, 46), Matty Taylor, Ellis Harrison (Jermaine Easter, 27)*
Substitutes: Jamie Lucas, Nathan Blissett, Danny Greenslade, Kieran Preston

9 *A guard of honour for Phil Kite's Testimonial*

1

■ ■ ■ The Memorial Stadium – Saturday 8th August 2015 ■ ■ ■

Bristol Rovers **0-1** Northampton Town

Referee: Mark Heywood
Attendance: 8,712

Goal: O'Toole (48)

There's something about the first day of a new football season that's quite unique.

No matter how good, or bad, your side's pre-season fixtures have been, the sense of anticipation as a new season dawns takes some beating.

And so it was, at least for me, on this sunny August Saturday as Rovers kicked off the 2015/16 campaign back in the Football League after a one season sojourn in the Vanarama Conference.

The visitors for our first game back in the league were Northampton Town, one of two other sides who might well have been relegated instead of us a little more than 12 months ago and in their squad were three players with Rovers connections.

John-Joe O'Toole was the most recent of those to have worn the colours of Rovers, having departed BS7 after relegation had been confirmed, under a little bit of a cloud following a somewhat critical newspaper interview he gave just prior to the last game of last season. Consequently, he was booed every time he went near the ball.

Goalkeeper Ryan Clarke, another ex-Rovers player, newly arrived at Northampton following a lengthy stint with Oxford United, had to be content with a place on the bench. Meanwhile The Cobblers skipper, Marc Richards, never kicked a ball in anger for Rovers, but trained with the club when Ian Atkins embarked on a mission to beat the number of players recruited by one manager in a single summer, this particular one being 2004.

As for Rovers, well Billy Bodin spent the second half of last season with Northampton, while Kaid Mohamed who had played for both clubs, was up in the stand watching after spending two days back training with Rovers as he looked to get himself fixed up with a club for the new season.

As for the game, it was a bit of a damp squib. A fairly even first half saw the visitors carve out a few chances while Matty Taylor, after intercepting a terrible back pass from Ryan Cresswell, somehow managed not to score with the goal at his mercy!

Inevitably the only goal of the game, when it arrived, was scored by O'Toole, arriving late to meet a cross into the box and glancing a header beyond Steve Mildenhall and into the net. The Rovers shot stopper then made two outstanding saves to deny Northampton further goals and although Ellis Harrison might have scored a Rovers equaliser in the final minutes, he hit the ball straight into the arms of grateful goalkeeper Adam Smith.

It was a disappointing opening day for the crowd of 8,712, but lessons will have been learned from defeat against a Northampton side who were a little bit more streetwise than Darrell Clarke's Rovers outfit.

 Bristol Rovers: *Mildenhall, Leadbitter, Clarke (J), Parkes, Brown, Sinclair, Lines, Lockyer, Montano (Monakana, 61), Taylor (Bodin, 71), Easter (Harrison, 56)*
Substitutes: Clarke (O), Gosling, Blissett, Preston

 Northampton Town: *Smith, Lelan, Diamond, Cresswell, Buchanan, Taylor, O'Toole (Hoskins, 73), Potter (Holmes, 64), Byron, Adams (Corry, 88), Richards*
Substitutes: McDonald, Calvert-Lewis, Hackett, Clarke

1 Rovers' substitutes for their first game back in the league, Nathan Blissett, Jeffrey Monakana, Billy Bodin, Jake Gosling, Ellis Harrison, Ollie Clarke and Kieran Preston

2 Matty Taylor rounds Northampton goalkeeper Adam Smith on his league debut

3 Chris Lines skippered the side on the opening day

4 Stuart Sinclair started where he left off last season, by winning the Man of the Match Award

5 Thumbs up for the start of the new campaign.

6 Lee Brown, in action at the start of an amazing season for him

7 Summer signing Cristian Montano is foiled by this challenge from John-Joe O'Toole

■ ■ ■ The Memorial Stadium – Tuesday 11th August 2015 – CC1 ■ ■ ■

Bristol Rovers **1-2** Birmingham City

Goal: Harrison (65)

Referee: Andy Davies
Attendance: 5,650

Goals: Maghoma (57), Shinnie (68)

Birmingham City's last visit to The Memorial Stadium had also been for a League Cup tie, on 11th September 2001.

The competition was then known as the Worthington Cup but the game will be remembered more for the date on which it was played than for the result or anything else that happened on the pitch that night.

Everyone was more focussed on the events that were happening in New York and Washington, and not on a football match in Bristol. All day long the horrific footage of the terrorist atrocities in America had unfolded on our television screens but those images had to be put to the back of the mind as the game kicked off.

Just for the record, the First Division outfit were far too strong for Rovers and recorded a convincing victory to ease through to the third round of the competition by virtue of a 3-0 win.

The only time the clubs had met since then was in an FA Cup tie at St Andrews back in January 2014 when The Blues were again 3-0 winners.

The most recent player to have turned out

for both sides was central defender Will Packwood who appeared in eight Rovers games when on loan from St Andrews in 2013. The American born defender was released by Birmingham in the summer and has returned to The States.

The only current connection on this occasion was former Blues player Kevan Broadhurst, who enjoyed a spell as assistant manager of Rovers under Ian Atkins. He seems to be quite an influential figure behind the scenes at his

Bristol Rovers: Mildenhall, Leadbitter, Clarke (J) (Broom, 81), Lockyer, Parkes, Brown, Sinclair, Clarke (O), Gosling (Montano, 64), Easter (Taylor, 64), Harrison
Substitutes: Blissett, Preston, Bodin, Malpas

Birmingham City: Legzdins, Eardley, Morrison (Spector, 71), Grounds, Robinson, Davis, Gleeson, Maghoma (Gray, 81), Shinnie, Novak, Thomas (Arthur, 90)
Substitutes: Donaldson, Cotterill, Brown, Kuszczak

former club and told me that he had been involved in the process of selecting current Brum manager Gary Rowett. His involvement in this game saw him behind the microphone, commentating on the match for Birmingham's website, but not before he had enjoyed a Memorial Stadium pastie which, he said, was a good reason on its own for coming to the match!

As for the game, Rovers put in a much improved performance following their opening day fixture against Northampton.

Darrell Clarke made three changes to his starting lineup, while Birmingham's Rowett made eight changes to his.

The visitors took a 56th minute lead through Jacques Maghoma, but Rovers hit back to equalise through Ellis Harrison just eight minutes later. However Andrew Shinnie beat Steve Mildenhall with a 20 yard shot three minutes later to claim the winner for Birmingham.

A positive performance from Rovers ended with a senior debut for Academy graduate Ryan Broom nine minutes from time.

1 The teams are out!
2 Jake Gosling challenges Paul Robinson
3 Tom Parkes comes face to face with Lee Novak
4 Having a drink at the bar!

5 Jermaine Easter is challenged by Paul Robinson
6 Ellis Harrison has just equalised...time to celebrate!
7 James Clarke takes on Jacques Maghoma

Yeovil Town **0-1** Bristol Rovers

Referee: Brendan Malone
Attendance: 5,895

Goal: Harrison (88)

Successive relegations for our hosts, coupled with our own promotion, saw us renew acquaintances with Yeovil Town after a short break.

Players who have turned out in the colours of both clubs are many, the most obvious one being a certain goalscorer by the name of Paul Randall. On this occasion, though, neither side included any players with experience of playing in green and white and blue and white.

Our last visit to Huish Park was four years ago when we registered a 1-0 win on 2nd April 2011. In that time very little has changed at the ground the Glovers call home.

The stadium is still very green in colour, the away terrace remains uncovered and the PA announcer still has the annoying (to me) habit of asking supporters in each stand to give a cheer before the match so that he can determine which area of the ground is the loudest.

It was a good job he asked the home fans beforehand, as they had absolutely nothing to cheer about during the entire 90 minutes!

Paul Sturrock's squad was light on numbers and he was only able to name five substitutes, one of whom was a goalkeeper while another, Jack Compton, apparently, wasn't really fit to play if he'd been required.

Rovers meanwhile included on loan Chesterfield goalkeeper Aaron Chapman in their starting lineup as manager Darrell Clarke revealed, beforehand, that he had told Steve Mildenhall that he was actively looking for a new first choice shot stopper.

Yeovil Town: *Krysiak, Roberts, Arthurworrey, Sokolik, Smith, Fogden, Dolan, Lacey, Cornick (Jeffers, 64), Beck (Burrows, 78), Bird*
Substitutes: Weale, Compton, Allen

Bristol Rovers: *Chapman, Leadbitter, Clarke (J), Lockyer (Montano, 75), Parkes, Brown, Lines, Clarke (O) (Monakana, 75), Sinclair, Taylor (Easter, 67), Harrison*
Substitutes: Gosling, Preston, Bodin, Malpas

One of the worst Yeovil sides I've seen struggled to cope with Clarke's outfit and the only surprise after 45 minutes was that the game remained goalless. That it did was entirely down to goalkeeper Artur Krysiak who made outstanding saves from Ellis Harrison (twice), James Clarke, Ollie Clarke and Matty Taylor (there were others, but those were the best).

Just after half time Chapman was called into action for the first and only time that afternoon and he did well to hold on to a low shot from Matthew Dolan, who had been booked for encroaching at a free kick in the first half.

He received a second yellow after bringing down Daniel Leadbitter and although the ten men held out until two minutes from the end of the match, they could do nothing to keep out Harrison's cracking left foot drive that sealed a Rovers victory.

Krysiak was beaten at last and Rovers claimed their first three point haul of the new campaign wearing their new yellow away strip.

The season was up and running and Harrison was able to claim our first league goal of the new campaign.

1 Rovers players arrive at Huish Park

2 Goalscorer Ellis Harrison is challenged by Stephen Arthurworrey

3 Time for a pie and a coffee before the game

4 Stuart Sinclair, Cristian Montano, Lee Brown and Chris Lines help Ellis Harrison celebrate his late strike

5 Stuart Sinclair gets past Matthew Dolan

6 Daniel Leadbitter is sandwiched between Jacub Sokalik and Wes Fogden

7 Goalkeeper Aaron Chapman warms up before making his Rovers debut

Luton Town **0-1** Bristol Rovers

Referee: Trevor Kettle
Attendance: 8,061

Goal: Sinclair (90)

Luton Town's Kenilworth Road is, like The Memorial Stadium, in need of a makeover or a bulldozer.

However as both clubs strive to obtain a move to a new ground, they have to make do and mend with their existing facility.

A bank of 24 glass fronted executive boxes runs the length of one side of the ground and the home and away dugouts are located on the same side. The stand behind one goal houses the home fans while away fans are seated behind the other. Press facilities, Directors Box and more Luton fans are on the opposite side to the Executive Boxes in an old wooden stand.

Entry for visiting press is through a gap in a row of terraced houses that surround the ground, where everyone has to walk underneath the bedroom of one of them!

After arriving at the hotel close to Luton airport to drop the players for their pre-match meal, there was a mechanical failure with the coach (the door wouldn't shut!) so four members of staff commandeered four taxis to take them and the kit to the ground.

The players arrived an hour or so later in a fleet of six taxis, while a mechanic from the coach company was called out to fix the faulty door.

Luton manager, John Still, enjoyed a spell as assistant manager of Rovers during Ray Graydon's time in charge. One of football's gentlemen Still, who has the unique distinction of leading three clubs out of The Conference into the Football League, extended a warm welcome to all connected with The Gas.

 Luton Town: *Tyler, O'Donnell, Wilkinson, Cuthbert, McNulty, Griffiths, Doyle (Smith, 65), McCourt, McGeehan (Ruddock, 70), Mackail-Smith (Marriott, 75), Benson*
Substitutes: Potts, Lawless, Justham, McQuoid

 Bristol Rovers: *Chapman, Leadbitter, Clarke (J), Lockyer, Parkes, Brown, Sinclair, Clarke (O), Lines, Harrison, Easter (Taylor, 68)*
Substitutes: Mildenhall, Gosling, Montano, Bodin, Malpas, Monakana

---

In the Rovers side was Stuart Sinclair, released by Luton some ten years before without making a first team appearance and desperate to play in this game.

Although Luton were a stronger side than the Yeovil outfit beaten so convincingly just a few days before, it made no difference as Rovers again played at a high tempo their hosts found it difficult to cope with.

Home goalkeeper Mark Tyler made one outstanding save from Lee Brown before the break and Rovers continued to dominate for much of the second half, so much so that Luton didn't force their first corner of the game until the 70th minute.

In fact the hosts didn't register a shot on target all evening and fell behind when the aforementioned Sinclair ran on to an exquisite pass from Matty Taylor to net the winning goal deep into stoppage time.

It was no more than Rovers deserved and he, his team mates, and Rovers supporters just had time to celebrate before the final whistle!

1 Rovers players celebrate Stuart Sinclair's winner

2 Confident before kick off!

3 Daniel Leadbitter is challenged by Scott Griffiths

4 Lee Brown shields the ball from Scott Cuthbert

5 Chris Lines takes on Cameron McGeehan

6 Ellis Harrison gets a shot away

7 Manager Darrell Clarke congratulates goalscorer Stuart Sinclair at the final whistle

■ ■ ■ The Memorial Stadium – Saturday 22nd August 2015 ■ ■ ■

Bristol Rovers **3-1** Barnet

Goals: Brown (2), Easter (77), Taylor (87)

Referee: Ross Joyce
Attendance: 7,107

Goal: Weston (85)

The side that beat Rovers to The Vanarama Conference title last season provided the opposition for our second home league game of the season.

Martin Allen was still in charge, though with the title of Head Coach as opposed to manager while his newly installed assistant was none other than former Rovers midfielder Gary Waddock, appointed to Allen's staff just 24 hours earlier.

John Akinde, former Bristol City striker and Rovers loanee and last season's top scorer in the country's fifth division, was booed every time he touched the ball with reference being made to his stint at Ashton Gate on more than one occasion. The fact that he couldn't hit a barn door when he was with us probably had a lot to do with it as well!

There were a few firsts on an afternoon when over 7,000 supporters turned up at The Memorial Stadium. Manager Darrell Clarke named an unchanged side for the first time, Lee Mansell was back in the squad for the first time since picking up a calf injury during pre-season and there was a first home game for on loan goalkeeper Aaron Chapman.

Barnet included their new signing Aaron McLean, though the lack of a pre-season told on him and he was substituted at half time.

By then Rovers were in front thanks to a well worked corner routine that saw Chris Lines find Lee Brown in acres of space some 30 yards from goal. The defender tried his luck with a low shot and it was deflected past goalkeeper Graham Stack in only the second minute of the game.

Bristol Rovers: Chapman, Leadbitter (Gosling, 32), Clarke (J), Lockyer, Parkes, Brown, Sinclair, Clarke (O), Lines, Harrison (Taylor, 61), Easter (Bodin, 84)
Substitutes: Mildenhall, Mansell, Montano, Monakana

Barnet: Stack, Hoyte (Muggleton, 74), Dembele, N'Gala, Johnson, Vilhete (Batt, 61), Weston, Togwell, Gambin, Akinde, McLean (Gash, 46)
Substitutes: Nelson, Tomlinson, Champion, Stephens

Two days later Brown's fellow defender Tom Parkes told anyone who would listen that the deflection came off of him and, after watching the replay he may well have had a point. Quite why he waited that long to claim it is a mystery, and the goal remains credited to Brown!

Jermaine Easter doubled the lead for Clarke's side with just 12 minutes remaining, but Curtis Weston pulled a goal back for the visitors on 86 minutes to set up what everyone thought might be a nervous finish. It was the first goal that Chapman had conceded since moving to The Mem.

The nervous finale didn't materialise as another first was achieved when Matty Taylor went straight down the other end and scored his first ever goal in the Football League.

Nine points in a week, a sweet victory against Barnet and a move up to fourth place in the League Two table made for a great afternoon.

!

1 Celebrating Lee Brown's second minute goal
2 Matty Taylor shields the ball from Bira Dembele
3 Jermaine Easter on the ball
4 Stuart Sinclair goes down under a heavy challenge

5 Daniel Leadbitter challenges Luke Gamblin
6 Tom Parkes keeps a close eye on the ball
7 Killing time waiting for the game to begin

1

Leyton Orient **2-0** Bristol Rovers

Goals: James (pen, 23), Simpson (45)

Referee: Darren Drysdale
Attendance: 5,777

Rovers travelled to East London hoping to preserve a proud away record, having not lost a league match on their travels since defeat at Braintree on 6th September 2014.

Darrell Clarke's side had gone 21 games without defeat, on that awful day in deepest, darkest, Essex. Include the play off semi final against Forest Green Rovers and the Promotion Final against Grimsby Town, then they could claim an unbeaten run of 23.

Rovers last played a league game at Brisbane Road on 12th February 2011 and on that occasion they went down 4-1, with a certain Harry Kane scoring twice for the O's after replacing the future Rovers striker Scott McGleish in the second half.

There were, however, no connections between the sides for this clash, the 111th meeting of the clubs in all competitions.

Clarke was forced into making one change to his starting lineup as hamstring victim Daniel Leadbitter missed out. As one door closed, though, another opened and so it was for first year pro Tyler Lyttle who was handed his Rovers, and League, debut.

The son of former Nottingham Forest and West Bromwich Albion player Des, the young defender is a former schoolboy international who was released by Wolves as a 16 year old. He took a year out after that to concentrate on his education before joining Rovers as a second year scholar. He became the second first year pro to be handed his senior debut this season, after Ryan Broom.

Looking around the ground, one could be forgiven for thinking that Rovers could, by now, be playing in a very similar

Leyton Orient: Cisak, Clohesy, Essam, Baudry (Dunne, 46), Shaw, James, Pritchard (Turgott, 79), Moore, Cox, Simpson (Palmer, 70), McCallum
Substitutes: Kashket, Maguire, Grainger, Moncur

Bristol Rovers: Chapman, Lyttle (Monakana, 46), Clarke (J), Lockyer, Parkes, Brown, Sinclair, Clarke (O) (Montano, 46) (Taylor, 60), Lines, Easter, Harrison
Substitutes: Mildenhall, Mansell, Gosling, Bodin

stadium as it was on Brisbane Road that the revamped Memorial Stadium was going to be modelled, with blocks of flats situated in each corner of the ground. Sadly, as we all know, those plans never came to fruition.

For the game, it's probably best forgotten as Rovers lost their unbeaten league record. Both Orient goals came in the opening 45 minutes. On 23 minutes Lyttle was judged to have fouled Paul McCallum in the area and Bristolian (and City fan!) Lloyd James sent Aaron Chapman the wrong way with the resulting spot kick.

The second arrived on the stroke of half time when Jay Simpson showed a decent first touch when receiving the ball in the area and slotting it past Chapman.

Rovers, who had looked lacklustre in the opening period, improved after the break and might, on another day, have got back on level terms, but this really was an uncharacteristic and lethargic performance by Clarke's side.

1 Rovers players acquaint themselves with the Brisbane Road pitch

2 Cristian Montano challenges Connor Essam

3 Jermaine Easter takes on Frazer Shaw

4 Tom Lockyer goes so close to pulling a goal back for Rovers

5 Thumbs up from these two!

6 Tyler Lyttle, pictured on his Rovers debut

7 Ellis Harrison is challenged by Sammy Moore

Bristol Rovers **0-1** Oxford United

Referee: James Linington
Attendance: 7,038

Goal: Roofe (62)

The international break meant that Sky were forced to dip into The Football League for their weekend's televised fixtures, with Rovers at home to Oxford chosen as a suitably attractive League Two match to show subscribers.

A 12.15pm kick off was the only downside, at least for those of us who had to work. The club were compensated for the inconvenient start time, although that was of little consequence for those who were impacted the most.

Connections between the clubs down the years are many, with several players having turned out for both sides.

On this occasion, Rovers fielded three former Oxford players, in the shape of James Clarke, Matty Taylor and Lee Mansell.

We last met Oxford in the relegation season of 2013/14 and it was at The Kassam Stadium that we recorded one of only two away wins all season.

The 47th league meeting of the sides was to see a win by the same scoreline, this time in favour of the U's, though that tells you nothing about the drama that unfolded during the 90 minutes.

Darrell Clarke's starting lineup saw two changes from the previous week, as Taylor came in for Ellis Harrison and Mansell started for the first time this season, having recovered from a calf injury. He replaced defender Tyler Lyttle.

The opening exchanges of the game saw two sides willing to get the ball down and pass it around but just when we were thinking we were in for a really good game of football referee James Linington

Bristol Rovers: Chapman, Sinclair, Clarke (J) (Bodin, 84), Lockyer, Parkes, Brown, Mansell (Montano, 73), Clarke (O), Lines, Taylor (Harrison, 67), Easter
Substitutes: Mildenhall, Greenslade, Lyttle, Monakana

Oxford United: Slocombe, Baldock, Wright, Dunkley, Skarz, Roofe (Lundstram, 76), Rose, Sercombe, MacDonald, Taylor (Hoban, 56), Hylton (Ruffels, 89)
Substitutes: Buchel, George, Roberts, Hawtin

decided he wanted to be the star of the show.

With just 17 minutes on the clock he decided to issue a straight red to Ollie Clarke following an aerial challenge on Danny Rose. It was the type of challenge seen in many games at all levels, yet the match official had the red card out of his pocket before the players fell to the ground!

Linington made a rod for his own back as the crowd, and Rovers players, were on his back all the time, urging cards to be brandished for every challenge.

The result was that he issued six yellow cards to the visitors, two of them to Liam Sercombe, who left the pitch after 59 minutes.

Three minutes later a wonder strike from Kemar Roofe beat Aaron Chapman and that was it, game over. Rovers did see a couple of decent opportunities comfortably saved by Sam Slocombe and they were denied a blatant penalty by the aforementioned match official when Billy Bodin was taken out.

The fact that Clarke's red card was rescinded three days later sums up Mr Linington's performance.

1 Rovers supporters arriving for the game
2 Stuart Sinclair challenges Joe Skarz
3 Matty Taylor is brought down by Cheyenne Dunkley
4 James Clarke fends off this challenge from Alex MacDonald

5 Chris Lines closes in as Joe Skarz clears
6 Killing time before kick off
7 Tom Parkes heads for goal

1

■ ■ ■ **The Memorial Stadium – Saturday 12th September 2015** ■ ■ ■

Bristol Rovers **0-1** Accrington Stanley

Referee: Kevin Johnson
Attendance: 6,351

Goal: Key (48)

A second home game in a week saw Accrington Stanley visit The Memorial Stadium for the first time since 28th January 2014.

On that occasion they had left Bristol with all three points after a last minute goal saw them register a fourth consecutive win against The Gas.

It had been a strange week as far as Rovers were concerned; following their Sunday afternoon defeat against Oxford United, they had reported back to The Mem the next day for the annual photoshoot minus two players.

The absence of Jeffrey Monakana was easy enough to explain as he had returned to Brighton & Hove Albion, his parent club, after appearing in just three games for Rovers, all from the bench.

The other absentee was former Manchester City youngster Adam Drury who, we were told, had left the club for personal reasons. The right sided midfielder/defender had only arrived at the club the previous Tuesday, so had never even kicked a ball for The Gas.

Two days before the game manager Darrell Clarke brought in another goalkeeper,

Wigan Athletic's Lee Nicholls, on a 93 day loan. The youngster who had previously enjoyed a loan spell with Accrington was to go straight into the squad in place of Aaron Chapman, another former Stanley loanee, who returned to his parent club, Chesterfield.

Nicholls duly made his debut between the posts and there was another first for Rovers as second year scholar Alfie Kilgour was named in the squad for the first time and took his place on the bench.

 Bristol Rovers: *Nicholls, Clarke (J), Lockyer, Parkes, Brown, Sinclair, Clarke (O) (Bodin, 77), Mansell (Gosling, 66), Lines, Harrison, Taylor (Easter, 72) Substitutes: Mildenhall, Montano, Lyttle, Kilgour*

 Accrington Stanley: *Mooney, Pearson, Winnard, Davies, Buxton, Crooks, Windass (Kee, 66), Conneely (Procter, 80), McConville (McCartan, 66), Mingoia, Gornell Substitutes: Etheridge, Barry, Wakefield, Bruna*

The visitors, who had played out a goalless draw at Portsmouth the previous week, wasted no time in making their intentions clear. They appeared to be happy with the point they already had and showed little as an attacking force. It has to be said, though, that they were a well organised outfit and every player stuck to his task throughout.

First half opportunities were few and far between, for both sides, and we reached half time with neither goalkeeper having had a serious shot to save.

It was a little bit more lively after the break, but neither side really looked as though they would break the deadlock and a goalless draw seemed an inevitable outcome until, that is, the 68th minute. From a corner on the right Billy Kee, just two minutes after coming on as a sub, somehow managed to score with a close range overhead kick.

Five minutes from time goalkeeper Jason Mooney touched a Chris Lines free kick round the post, while shortly afterwards Nicholls saved with his legs from McCartan. The visitors comfortably held out and celebrated with their 48 fans at the final whistle.

1 Ready for kick off

2 Ollie Clarke takes on Matt Crooks

3 Stuart Sinclair is 'cornered' by Adam Buxton

4 Billy Bodin keeps possession while Dean Winnard and Ellis Harrison look on

5 First time in the senior squad for Alfie Kilgour

6 Lee Brown shields the ball from Piero Mingoia

7 It's a cracking read!

■ ■ ■ **Home Park – Saturday 19th September 2015** ■ ■ ■

Plymouth Argyle **1-1** Bristol Rovers

Goal: Jervis (85)

Referee: Christopher Sarginson
Attendance: 10,633

Goal: Harrison (90, pen)

Rovers met Argyle for the 85th time in the league, though this was our first visit to the home of the Green Army for two years.

Back in September 2013 we were being told that the old wooden stand was to be demolished and a new one built to complete the refurbishment of the ground. However that hasn't happened and the old structure remains. Perched at the back of it during a game is very uncomfortable, as the wooden seats aren't the best and the view is obstructed by several well placed pillars!

There were familiar faces in the Plymouth squad, in the shape of Ryan Brunt who was on the bench for this game, and Gary Sawyer who had only recently returned for a second spell at the club, having played for Leyton Orient for three years after leaving Rovers in the summer of 2012.

There were Plymouth connections in the Rovers squad as well; Jermaine Easter played 36 games for The Greens after joining them initially on loan, back in October 2007. After the match I was asked for his contact details by the secretary/chairman of the Argyle Legends

organisation and when I made a comment that he could hardly be a legend after so few games, I was told that; "Anyone who pulls on an Argyle shirt is a legend." Put me in my place!

Paul Maxwell, Rovers physio, is also a former Argyle player and was also a member of the medical team at Home Park for some 11 years.

The game proved to be a great advert for League Two football. Goalless at the break, following an opening half when chances

Plymouth Argyle: : *McCormick, Mellor, Nelson, Hartley, Sawyer. McHugh, (Cox, 50), Tanner (Wylde, 62), Carey, Boateng, Reid (Brunt, 81), Jervis*
Substitutes: Simpson, Harvey (T), Purrington, Harvey(C)

Bristol Rovers: *Nicholls, Clarke (J), Lockyer, Parkes, Brown, Bodin, Sinclair, Lines, Gosling (Montano, 66), Taylor (Harrison, 69), Easter (Lucas, 87)*
Substitutes: Mildenhall, McChrystal, Mansell, Clarke (O)

were few and far between, both sides went all out for victory in the second half.

Lee Nicholls made one outstanding save from Jake Jervis on 57 minutes, but could do little to prevent the same player from opening the scoring on 85 minutes as he connected to a cross from the left to score from close range at the back post.

Thankfully, three minutes later Ellis Harrison was fouled by Plymouth keeper Luke McCormick and a penalty was awarded. Harrison grabbed the ball to take the spot kick but had to wait for what seemed like an eternity before he could take it. McCormick had to be treated following the injury he sustained in committing the foul and was then booked when he had fully recovered.

Harrison then despatched the penalty high into the roof of the net for a deserved equaliser before being denied a late winner when McCormick's reaction save from his close range header kept out what would have been a dramatic winning goal.

■ TWO TO ONE ■

1 Home Park, Plymouth

2 Jake Gosling is challenged by Jake Mellor

3 Ellis Harrison steps up to rifle home the equaliser from the penalty spot

4 Matty Taylor on the ball

5 Cristian Montano is challenged by Hiram Boateng

6 Jermaine Easter shields the ball from Graham Carey

7 Enjoying a sunny day at Home Park

■ ■ ■ The Memorial Stadium – Saturday 26th September 2015 ■ ■ ■

Bristol Rovers **1-2** Portsmouth

Goal: Easter (48)

Referee: Jeremy Simpson
Attendance: 8,555

Goals: Evans (29), Stockley (71)

The last time Portsmouth visited The Memorial Stadium they were deep in the financial mire and succumbed to John Ward's Rovers side who won 2-0.

Times have changed, though, and the club with the division's biggest budget arrived in Bristol as one of three unbeaten sides in the country, with Brighton and Leicester City being the other two.

Although there have been connections between the clubs down the years, the only one on this occasion was Pompey's goalkeeping coach Scott Bevan who played for Rovers in the Paul Buckle era.

Up in the press box I was sat next to Portsmouth legend Guy Whittingham who I once saw score four goals for the visitors against Rovers.

A crowd of over 8,500 turned up to see if Darrell Clarke's side could be the first to win against a revitalised Pompey whose supporters numbered 1,188. Unfortunately for them, they were to see their side make a change before the game had even kicked off, with Adam McGurk injured in the warm up and having to be replaced by Jayden Stockley, leaving the visitors one short on the bench.

Clarke named a side showing three changes from the previous week. Daniel Leadbitter returned after a four match lay off with a hamstring injury and there were also recalls for Ellis Harrison and Ollie Clarke. The players left out were Matty Taylor, Jake Gosling and Billy Bodin.

Although Rovers began brightly, the visitors soon showed why they have been so difficult to beat and it came as no surprise when they took a 29th minute lead.

Bristol Rovers: *Nicholls, Leadbitter, Clarke (J) (Gosling, 46), Lockyer, Parkes, Brown, Sinclair, Lines, Clarke (O) (Bodin, 46), Easter (Taylor, 72), Harrison*
Substitutes: Mildenhall, McChrystal, Mansell, Montano

Portsmouth: *McCarey, Davies, Burgess, Clarke, Stevens, Bennett (Naismith, 74), Barton, Hollands, Evans, Chaplin (Roberts, 68), Stockley (Tubbs, 69)*
Substitutes: Bass, Webster, May

Goalkeeper Lee Nicholls had already made a fine save from Gareth Evans but was soon beaten by the same player who headed past him following a cross from the right.

Portsmouth keeper Aaron McCarey, on loan from Wolves and making his Pompey debut, made an excellent reaction save to keep out a Jermaine Easter piledriver, but the visitors were still ahead at the break.

Easter did though manage to equalise three minutes into the second half, reacting first to a corner from the right to touch the ball in off the underside of the crossbar.

The same player saw another ferocious drive deflected on to a post and if Rovers had gone ahead at that point they might well have won the game.

However the aforementioned Stockley had the last laugh when he touched another cross from the right past Nicholls to wrap things up for his side. There was no spirited fightback on this occasion and a classy Portsmouth side easily held out to take all three points and a place at the top of the table.

1 *Steve Yates, Marcus Stewart and Darrell Clarke watch intently*

2 *Jermaine Easter celebrates his 48th minute equaliser*

3 *Matty Taylor is brought down by Christian Burgess*

4 *Ollie Clarke takes on Danny Hollands*

5 *James Clarke beats Jayden Stockley to the ball*

6 *Waiting for kick off*

7 *Billy Bodin on the attack*

Hartlepool United **0-3** Bristol Rovers

Referee: Darren Handley
Attendance: 3,788

Goals: Taylor (33), Bodin (64), Easter (78)

Every time we travel to Victoria Park to face Hartlepool, thoughts return to a glorious sunny day in May 2007 when Rovers recovered from a one goal deficit to win 2-1, deny their hosts the title and clinch a place in the promotion play offs.

I can still see a smiling Rickie Lambert, arms raised, stood in front of the Rovers supporters who had made the long trip to the north east. His winning goal had come near the end of a pulsating, if nervous, match.

The Hartlepool officials, generous in defeat, had allowed the Rovers players and staff to celebrate with the travelliing Gasheads before celebrating themselves, for although they hadn't clinched the title, they had secured one of the automatic promotion spots.

The last time the sides met at the same venue wasn't such a joyous occasion, more of an embarrassment in fact. John Ward's side were thrashed 4-0 much to the dismay of then assistant manager Darrell Clarke, a former Hartlepool player.

Clarke, now the man in charge of course, was returning to his former club for the first time as a manager on this autumnal evening. He wasn't the only man with Hartlepool connections returning to the club. Jermaine Easter made 29 appearances for 'Pool, all from the bench and in an interview ahead of the game had said that he didn't enjoy his time in the north east at all.

Clarke had spent six years as a player with the evening's hosts and spoke fondly of his time there. He still knows many people behind the scenes and received a generous round of applause from the home supporters when the sides came out to do battle. He even left Victoria Park with a framed photo of himself playing for the club some years ago.

He made five changes to his starting lineup following the previous weekend's defeat at the hands of Portsmouth, with the axe falling on Chris Lines, Tom Parkes, Ellis Harrison, Ollie Clarke and Daniel Leadbitter. They were replaced by skipper Mark McChrystal, in for his first game of the season after injury, Lee Mansell, Matty Taylor, Billy Bodin and Jake Gosling.

Clarke's rejuvenated lineup never looked like losing this one and after a scintillating first half that saw them take a single goal lead into the half time interval, they added two more goals after the break to cap a truly impressive performance.

Taylor opened the scoring on 33 minutes, while Bodin scored his first Rovers goal with 64 minutes on the clock. The third goal came, inevitably, from Easter who anticipated, and intercepted, a shocking back pass by substitute Kudus Oyenuga and raced on to slot the ball past Adam Bartlett.

Hartlepool United: *Bartlett, Halliday, Boyce, Harrison, Carroll, Featherstone, Bates (Magnay, 72), Walker (Oyenuga, 64), Oates, Paynter, Fenwick Substitutes: Hawkins, Jones, Nearney, Smith, Denton*

Bristol Rovers: *Nicholls, Clarke (J), Lockyer, McChrystal (Parkes, 83), Brown, Bodin (Clarke (O) 84), Sinclair, Mansell, Gosling, Easter (Harrison, 79), Taylor Substitutes: Mildenhall, Lines, Lucas, Montano*

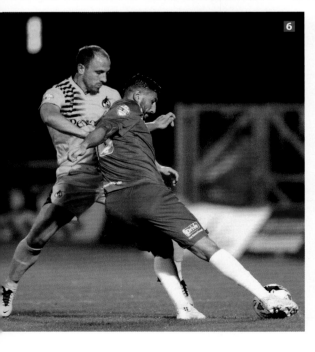

1 Some of the 190 Rovers supporters who made the long trek to Victoria Park

2 Darrell gets a hug from an old friend!

3 Lee Mansell gets to the ball ahead of Matthew Bates

4 Billy Bodin gets a shot away

5 Matty Taylor opens the scoring

6 Mark McChrystal challenges Billy Paynter

7 Jermaine Easter has just scored against his former club

■ ■ ■ **The Globe Arena – Saturday 3rd October 2015** ■ ■ ■

Morecambe **3-4** Bristol Rovers

Goals: Miller (44), Barkhuizen (60), Mullin (pen, 88)

Referee: Andrew Madeley
Attendance: 1,712

Goals: Mansell (28), Bodin (47), Taylor (59), Harrison (pen, 80)

A second long trip in a matter of days was the prospect for Darrell Clarke and his side as they set off for Morecambe just over 48 hours after returning from Hartlepool.

On this occasion they were afforded the comparative luxury of an overnight stay at a hotel some 30 miles from the ground.

Connections between Rovers and Morecambe are few and far between; in fact I can only recall one player, Craig Stanley, turning out for both sides, although Morecambe's current goalkeeping coach Lee Jones is a former Rovers player.

This was our fourth visit to Morecambe's Globe Arena, still a relatively new venue; the club moved to the ground some five years ago. It's what I would describe as functional and built for purpose with one main stand, covered terracing behind each goal, and a rather shallow terrace running the length of the pitch opposite the stand.

The club doesn't attract high crowds, and for this game the decision was taken not to open one of the covered terraces, so the game was, in effect, played in a three sided ground. Still, the playing surface was good and everyone behind the scenes really friendly.

The Rovers boss had the rare luxury of naming an unchanged side for the game, hardly surprising given the way they played against Hartlepool just a few days earlier.

The only change was on the bench where Daniel Leadbitter came in for Jamie Lucas,

Morecambe: *Roche, Parrish, Dugdale, Edwards, Beeley, Fleming, Goodall (Kenyon, 71), Barkhuizen, Devitt (Mullin, 80), Molyneux (Ellison, 71), Miller*
Substitutes: McGowan, Bailey, Thompson, Ryan

Bristol Rovers: *Nicholls, Clarke (J), Lockyer, McChrystal, Brown, Bodin (Leadbitter, 88), Sinclair, Mansell, Gosling, Easter (Harrison, 74), Taylor (Clarke (O), 82)*
Substitutes: Mildenhall, Parkes, Lines, Montano

now in a second loan spell with Boreham Wood.

Looking comfortable from the off, Rovers took a 28th minute lead through Lee Mansell, his first goal of the season, but conceded an equaliser a minute before half time when Lee Nicholls had a rush of blood to the head and raced to the edge of the area in an attempt to prevent Shaun Miller scoring. He needn't have bothered as the Morecambe man had time and space to chip the ball over him and into an empty net.

The second half was a veritable goalfest, as Billy Bodin and Matty Taylor gave Rovers a two goal cushion before Tom Barkhuizen pulled a goal back for the home side.

Ellis Harrison's penalty, his third spot kick for the club after entering the fray as a substitute, restored the two goal advantage before Paul Mullin converted a late penalty for the home side to make Rovers supporters suffer an anxious final few minutes.

And so, in a week that saw them travel 978 miles, Rovers returned to Bristol with six points and seven goals in the bag.

1. Lee Mansell scores his first goal of the season
2. Matty Taylor fends off a challenge from Adam Dugdale
3. It was the day that Steve Yates handed over kit manager duties to Marco Carota
4. Stuart Sinclair and Adam Dugdale in a race for the ball
5. Time for a quick snap!
6. Billy Bodin keeps Shaun Beeley at bay
7. Tom Lockyer keeps a close eye on Shaun Miller

■ ■ The Memorial Stadium – Tuesday 6th October 2015 – JPT 2 ■ ■

Bristol Rovers **2-0** Wycombe Wanderers

Goals: Taylor (4), Easter (11)

Referee: Oliver Langford
Attendance: 3,243

Rovers met Wycombe Wanderers for the fifth time in the Football League Trophy, now known as the Johnstone's Paint Trophy.

Johnstone's Paint are celebrating ten years of sponsoring this competition, and the advert provided by them for the programme was a painful reminder that Rovers had lost the first ever final under their jurisdiction as the company showed an image of the victorious Doncaster Rovers skipper with the Trophy in 2007. Doncaster, of course, beat Rovers 3-2 in the final played at the Millennium Stadium in Cardiff.

Rovers beat Wycombe on their way to the final that season, when one of their two goals was scored by Jamal Easter, brother of Jermaine who was in the Wycombe lineup that evening.

Moving swiftly on to the present day and Jermaine, of course, is now an integral member of Rovers current squad and he wasn't the only player on view who has turned out for both clubs.

Wycombe skipper Joe Jacobson is a former Rovers player though he was left on the bench for this clash as both managers made changes for the match.

Darrell Clarke made four in total, mainly enforced, as Jake Gosling and Tom Lockyer were away on international duty. He also rested Lee Mansell and James Clarke and recalled Daniel Leadbitter, Chris Lines, Cristian Montano and Tom Parkes.

A larger than expected crowd turned up for the game and they were treated to an outstanding and entertaining game of football, with both sides attacking at every opportunity.

Bristol Rovers: *Nicholls, Leadbitter, Parkes, McChrystal, Brown, Bodin, Lines, Sinclair (Clarke (O), 74), Montano (Lyttle, 90), Easter (Blissett, 88), Taylor*
Substitutes: Mildenhall, Kilgour

Wycombe Wanderers: *Ingram, Jombati, Pierre, Rowe, Sellers (O'Nein, 73), Banton, Bloomfield, McGinn, Wood, Kretzschmar (Jacobson, 88), Amadi-Holloway (Thompson, 88)*
Substitutes: Lynch, Ugwu

There were so many chances created during the ninety minutes that it was strange the only two goals of the evening came in the opening 11 minutes.

Just four minutes had elapsed when Matty Taylor showed a great touch to bring down a high ball from Chris Lines and cut inside before curling a stunning shot into the top right hand corner of the net to register his third goal in successive games.

His strike partner, Easter, also got in on the act with 11 minutes on the clock, scoring his third goal in four games when he was played in by Billy Bodin before rifling a ferocious angled drive past goalkeeper Matt Ingram.

In between the goals Wycombe's Aaron Pierre had headed against the crossbar and Lee Nicholls had done well to save Matt Bloomfield's close range effort from the rebound.

The opening period set the tone for the entire 90 minutes as both sides counter attacked at will but in spite of the many chances and an outstanding second half display by Ingram, who saved well from Montano, Bodin and Easter in particular, there were no further goals.

1 Red sky at night...Rovers delight?

2 Matty Taylor gets a shot away

3 Tom Parkes went close to scoring with this effort

4 Jermaine Easter is chased by Aaron Pierre and Sido Jombati

5 Billy Bodin gets in a cross

6 Stuart Sinclair takes on Stephen McGinn

7 Darrell Clarke enjoys a pre-match chat with Gareth Ainsworth

1

Mansfield Town **1-2** Bristol Rovers

Goal: Tafazolli (81)

Referee: Stephen Martin
Attendance: 6,743

Goals: Easter (15), Taylor (90)

It's some two years since Rovers last paid a visit to what I'll always refer to as Field Mill to take on Mansfield Town, the side that despatched us to The Conference on 3rd May 2014.

Mansfield's ground now goes by the name of The One Call Stadium and we were told, in no uncertain terms, to make sure we called it that at all times!

Entering the dressing room area we were confronted by some familiar faces, at least those of us with long memories were! Scott Shearer, Reggie Lambe and Chris Beardsley, all formerly of the parish of Horfield, are now plying their trade with The Stags.

All the Mansfield players were resplendent in club suits and ties and looked very very smart. I don't recall any other club providing matchday suits for their players; possibly due to cost and the seasonal turnover of players.

A giant plaque inside the stand that houses the press box declares that the ground was established on the site in 1861 and is officially the oldest ground in the Football league. Bet it was called Field Mill back then!

Darrell Clarke made three changes for the match, and selected James Clarke, Tom Lockyer and Lee Mansell in place of Mark McChrystal, Cristian Montano and Billy Bodin.

Rovers soaked up a great deal of early pressure, but took a 15th minute lead when Matty Taylor's cross from the right was chested into the path of Jermaine Easter by Daniel Leadbitter (goodness knows

Mansfield Town: *Jensen, Hunt, Pearce, Tafazolli, Benning, Lambe (Thomas (N), 55), Chapman, McGuire (Clements, 55), Westcarr, Green, Thomas (J) (Yussuf, 51)*
Substitutes: Shearer, Rose, Collins, Blair

Bristol Rovers: *Nicholls, Leadbitter, (Harrison, 46), Clarke (J), Lockyer, Parkes, Brown, Mansell (Gosling, 84), Lines (Clarke (O) (46), Sinclair, Easter, Taylor*
Substitutes: Mildenhall, McChrystal Montano, Blissett

what he was doing in the opposition penalty area!) and lashed into the roof of the net by the former Welsh international.

Easter, though, was both yellow and red carded in time added on at the end of the first half. The yellow was for diving, the red for an alleged head butt, though quite how referee saw it as that was unbelievable, as video evidence proved, and the red card was rescinded three days later.

The second half saw things evened up as first of all the home side's Krystian Pearce was sent off for manhandling Tom Lockyer as they waited for a free kick to be taken and then home skipper Nicky Hunt was dismissed after collecting two yellow cards.

Amazingly the nine men equalised through Ryan Tafazolli with nine minutes remaining, but the drama wasn't over as in the eighth minute of added time Matty Taylor headed home a perfect cross from James Clarke to make it four wins on the spin for Clarke's side.

1 Waiting for battle to commence

2 Jermaine Easter on his way to opening the scoring

3 It's fair to say that it was quite a physical encounter!

4 Matty Taylor scores the last gasp winner

5 James Clarke and Adi Yusuf go toe to toe!

6 Ollie Clarke is tackled by Chris Clements

7 Dom, the Gashead from Stoke, with his partner Ann - a home game for them...almost!

■ ■ ■ The Memorial Stadium – Tuesday 20th October 2015 ■ ■ ■

Bristol Rovers **0-0** Notts County

Referee: Stephen Martin
Attendance: 6,743

The country's oldest football club, Notts County, pitched up at The Memorial Stadium for the first time since September 2010 for the 83rd league meeting between the sides.

Our sojourn in The Conference meant that last season there were two divisions between us, but our promotion and their relegation meant that once again we were able to resume hostilities with the men from Meadow Lane.

A new manager, Dutchman Ricardo Moniz, had taken charge in April, too late to help The Magpies avoid the drop, but soon enough to prepare them for life in League Two.

There were some well known faces in the County squad, Northern Irish international goalkeeper Roy Carroll, former England, Leeds United and Manchester United striker Alan Smith, and ex Bristol City striker Jon Stead to name but three from a squad of 38!

Darrell Clarke made four changes to his starting lineup, bringing in Mark McChrystal, Jake Gosling, Billy Bodin and Ellis Harrison in place of Tom Parkes, James Clarke, Jermaine Easter and Chris Lines.

Gone are the days when managers would keep the same team after winning four games on the spin, it truly is a squad game these days!

It's not only squads that change, formations do as well. Rovers, for example, opted to start this game playing 4-4-2, while County employed a midfield diamond, in which Smith was the focal point.

Given the County manager's nationality, it wasn't surprising that his side liked to keep

---

 Bristol Rovers: *Nicholls, Leadbitter, Lockyer, McChrystal, Brown, Bodin (Montano, 71), Sinclair, Mansell, Gosling, Taylor (Blissett, 71), Harrison (Easter, 46)*
Substitutes: Mildenhall, Parkes, Clarke (O), Lines

 Notts County: *Carroll, Hewitt, Edwards, Sheehan, Audel (Amevor, 71), Aborah, Smith, Noble, Thompson (Campbell, 46), Mcleod, Stead*
Substitutes: Loach, Barmby, Burke, Jenner, Swerts

---

possession as much as possible. In the first half of this encounter, they played very deep, almost inviting Rovers to counter attack but although Clarke's side played an attractive brand of football, they only carved out a few real goalscoring opportunities.

McChrystal volleyed just wide of the mark early on, and was therefore forced to extend his wait for a first league goal for The Gas, and Lee Brown forced Carroll into an unorthodox looking save from his long range effort.

The best chance of the half, though, arrived late on when Bodin lashed a tremendous shot against the bar and saw it come back into play before being cleared.

The second half was a fairly even affair, and although County came out of their shell a little bit more, they weren't too adventurous and didn't register a single shot on target all night.

With a little bit more guile in front of goal, Rovers might have sealed a fifth straight win, but as it was they had to be content with a point from their first goalless draw since the one at Macclesfield in March.

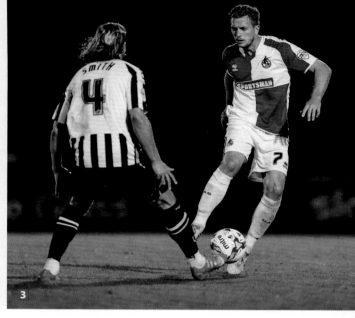

1 *The teams come out on to The Memorial Stadium pitch*
2 *Billy Bodin tries to get past Elliot Hewitt*
3 *Lee Mansell takes on Alan Smith*
4 *Bit of a Mexican wave going on here!*

5 *Mark McChrystal is challenged by Izale McLeod.*
6 *Stuart Sinclair prepares to tackle Liam Noble*
7 *Jake Gosling is stopped in his tracks by Stanley Arborah*

1

Bristol Rovers **1-4** Newport County

Goal: Bodin (15)

Referee: Nicholas Kinseley
Attendance: 7,442

Goals: Parkes (og, 13), Ansah (52 &56), O'Sullivan (76)

It seemed strange that, in this latest instalment of what has been dubbed a Severnside derby, there were no players on duty who had turned out for both clubs.

Bottom of the table Newport arrived in Bristol with just two wins to their name all season, both of them recorded away from home, at Carlisle and, just four days earlier, at Wycombe.

This was to be their fifth game under recently appointed manager John Sheridan, who had taken over from former England international Terry Butcher.

Rovers were looking to boost their home results, which made for quite dismal reading as only four points had been gained from the six games at The Memorial Stadium to date, while the same number of games on the road had yielded 16 points.

Manager Darrell Clarke's hand was forced in terms of team selection as skipper Mark McChrystal picked up an ankle injury in training just two days before this game, and Ellis Harrison was still nursing a slight hamstring strain picked up in the midweek game against Notts County, although he was deemed fit enough to

take his place on the bench.

Their places went to Tom Parkes and Jermaine Easter respectively, though in the case of the former he probably wished he hadn't been involved at all as he enjoyed a torrid day at the office!

With just 13 minutes on the clock, the central defender inadvertently gave the visitors the lead when he headed past his own goalkeeper.

He would have been delighted, no doubt, that two minutes later team mate Billy

Bristol Rovers: *Nicholls, Leadbitter, Lockyer, Parkes, Brown, Bodin, Sinclair, Mansell (Lines, 57), Gosling (Montano, 57), Taylor, Easter (Harrison, 73)*
Substitutes: Mildenhall, Clarke (O), Clarke (J), Blissett

Newport County: *Day, Donacien, Bennett, Partridge, Barnum-Bobb, Barrow (Holmes, 88), O'Sullivan (Klukowski, 80), Byrne, Elito, John-Lewis, Ansah (Boden, 83)*
Substitutes: Taylor (R), Taylor (M), Rodman, Collins

Bodin got him out of jail on this occasion when he hit a stunning volley past goalkeeper Joe Day who was left grasping at thin air as the striker's effort nestled in the back of the net.

From then until half time Rovers bossed the game and Stuart Sinclair and Matty Taylor went close to putting Clarke's side ahead. There was certainly no hint of what was to come after the break.

Seven minutes in, though, goalkeeper Lee Nicholls inexplicably dropped the ball at the feet of Zak Ansah who was able to walk the ball into an empty net.

The Newport man scored again four minutes after his first, as he got the better of Parkes and lashed a 25 yard shot past Nicholls.

The unfortunate Parkes then managed to direct a header from a corner on to the Newport crossbar, but Rovers' misery was compounded 14 minutes from time when Tommy O'Sullivan scored with a shot from the edge of the box.

1 Newport on the attack

2 Jermaine Easter is challenged by Janoi Donacien

3 Cristian Montano on the ball

4 Lee Brown comes face to face with Jazzi Barnum-Bobb

5 Matty Taylor is beaten to the ball by Medy Elito

6 Billy Bodin is closed down by Scott Barrow

7 Brothers in Arms!

Cambridge United **1-2** Bristol Rovers

Goal: Corr (33)

Referee: Brendan Malone
Attendance: 5,115

Goals: Harrison (66), Taylor (83)

The last time Rovers visited The Abbey Stadium was back in October 2004 and very little has changed in that time.

Getting to Cambridge on a Friday turned out to be a nightmare, and it was just shy of five hours from Bristol to the team hotel, though that did take in a 30 minute stop to repair the skylight on the coach, which had threatened to blow off as we headed up the M4!

Players just had time for a pre-match meal before setting out for the Abbey Stadium, best described in the following way.

Behind one goal is a smart all seater stand that was then, and still is, used for away supporters, while behind the other goal is a terrace used by home fans.

There is another terrace running the length of the pitch on one side of the ground and an all seater stand opposite, which also houses the dressing rooms and corporate facilities.

It is, though, a tired old ground in need of some modernisation, just like The Mem!

Whenever I go back to the stadium I can't forget the game between the sides on 21st December 2002 when the home side recorded a 3-1 victory that ensured Rovers spent Christmas at the foot of the League Two table. It was also the occasion on which Bradley Allen scored his only Rovers goal.

Manager Darrell Clarke made three changes to his starting lineup following the previous weekend's heavy defeat at the hands of Newport County, recalling James Clarke, Ellis Harrison and Mark McChrystal in place of Daniel Leadbitter, Matty Taylor and Tom Parkes.

Cambridge United: *Dunn, Sesay, Taylor, Roberts, Dunk, Donaldson (Newton, 84), Hughes (L) (Gaffney, 69), Berry, Hughes (J), Corr, Simpson (Demitriou, 69) Substitutes: Omozusi, Slew, Beasant, Coulson*

Bristol Rovers: *Nicholls, Clarke (J), Lockyer, McChrystal, Brown, Bodin, Sinclair, Mansell, Gosling, Easter (Taylor, 62), Harrison Substitutes: Mildenhall, Leadbitter, Parkes, Clarke (O), Lines, Montano*

The first half was a fairly low key affair, though the home side led by a solitary goal at the break following a lapse of concentration at the back by Rovers.

A good run down the left by Harrison Dunk ended with a perfect cross to the back post that found the unmarked Barry Corr and he planted a firm header beyond the reach of goalkeeper Lee Nicholls.

Rovers were out of the blocks quickly at the start of the second half and an Ellis Harrison header grazed the crossbar before the youngster put his side back on level terms, snapping up a loose ball after goalkeeper Chris Dunn had parried a shot from Matty Taylor into his path.

Taylor, who had started the game on the bench, certainly livened up proceedings and it was fitting that he scored the winning goal some seven minutes from time when he intercepted Greg Taylor's shockingly underhit back pass, ran on and rounded Dunn before rolling the ball into an empty net.

1. Chris Lines, Ollie Clarke, Cristian Montano and Daniel Leadbitter get the Abbey habit!
2. Tom Lockyer heads for goal
3. Matty Taylor shields the ball

4. Jake Gosling takes on Ryan Donaldson
5. Rovers fans celebrate
6. Lee Brown faces Liam Hughes
7. Ellis Harrison is challenged by Greg Taylor

■ ■ The Memorial Stadium – Sunday 8th November 2015 – FAC 1 ■ ■

Bristol Rovers **0-1** Chesham United

Referee: Andy Davies
Attendance: 5,181

Goal: Blake (77)

A home tie against non league Chesham United in this season's first round FA Cup tie afforded Darrell Clarke's side an opportunity of at least progressing to the next stage of the competition.

The game had been moved to a Sunday to give BBC the opportunity of what they call single camera coverage, which means one camera covering the game so that goal reports and incidents can be relayed back to the studio and shown almost immediately on screen.

Inconvenient, yes, but money talks and both sides picked up an extra £12,000 each for the move to The Sabbath.

The so called romance of the FA Cup was alive and kicking for this tie as former Rovers striker Barry Hayles had been appointed as player coach of our opponents back in the summer and the possibility of him playing against the club where it all began for him was a major talking point.

Remembrance Sunday meant that a one minute silence was observed before the match and a Guard of Honour, provided by our old friends from 21st Signal Regiment,

Azimghur Barracks, Colerne, made for a moving spectacle.

Rovers made two changes to their starting lineup, with Matty Taylor and Daniel Leadbitter coming in for Jermaine Easter and James Clarke.

When the game got underway, there was a nervous 30 minutes or so for Darrell Clarke's side, during which they survived a missed penalty.

Bristol Rovers: *Nicholls, Leadbitter (Clarke (J), 73), Lockyer, McChrystal, Brown, Bodin, Mansell (Lines, 62), Sinclair, Gosling, Harrison, Taylor (Easter, 62)*
Substitutes: Mildenhall, Parkes, Lucas, Montano

Chesham United: *Gore, Fenton, Ujah, Beasant, Little, Smith, Youngs, Taylor (Hamilton-Forbes, 90), Pearce (Hayles, 72), Blake (Casey, 86), Wadkins*
Substitutes: Legg, Fongho, Fletcher, Woodcock

Tom Lockyer was adjudged to have fouled Brad Wadkins in the area, but goalkeeper Lee Nicholls dived full length to touch Dave Pearce's spot kick round the post.

It seemed to be the wake up call needed by Rovers and they went close to scoring on a couple of occasions before the break though Matty Taylor's header, which was cleared off the line, was as good as it got.

Clarke's side laid siege to the Chesham goal in the second half but in spite of their efforts they were unable to pierce a determined opposition rearguard. That, and a tendency to take one touch too many when finding themselves in good positions, was to cost them dearly.

Hayles was introduced as a substitute on 72 minutes and the winning goal arrived five minutes later when Ryan Blake was allowed the freedom of the left flank before he drilled a shot under the despairing dive of Nicholls.

The romance of the FA Cup is all well and good but when your side is on the wrong end of a result such as this it's not nice!

It was the first time that Rovers had lost a home FA Cup tie to non league opposition.

1 An impeccably observed one minute's silence on Remembrance Sunday

2 Barry Hayles goes on as a 72nd minute substitute

3 Jake Gosling wins this aerial challenge

4 Lee Nicholls saves Toby Little's penalty

5 Lee Mansell closes in on Brad Wadkins

6 Stuart Sinclair outpaces Brad Wadkins

7 Support from above!

■ ■ Roots Hall – Wednesday 11th November 2015 – JPT Qtr Final ■ ■

Southend United 1-0 Bristol Rovers

Goal: White (11)

Referee: Andy Woolmer
Attendance: 3,337

A return to Roots Hall, after an absence of just over two years, came on a mild Wednesday night in November.

League One side Southend United hosted this Football League Trophy match, the fifth time that they and Rovers have done battle in the competition and The Shrimpers have yet to lose in this mini series.

Like Rovers, Southend have been hoping to move to a new stadium for a number of years. Indeed some years ago they proudly displayed a 3D model of their new venue close to the reception area. The model is still there, gathering dust in a passageway off of the entrance to the dressing rooms and they seem no closer to getting their new ground than they were ten years ago.

Consequently it appears that very little cash is being spent on what is an increasingly dilapidated stadium which houses an odd two tier stand for home fans behind one goal.

Behind the scenes the visitors dressing room is no bigger than a broom cupboard; certainly it has the dubious distinction of being the smallest in League Two!

There were two familiar faces in the Southend squad in former Rovers skipper Adam Barrett, still going strong at 36 and central defender Cian Bolger.

Barrett played in this game, his first after six weeks out through injury, while Bolger was dropped, though he preferred to use the word rested!

Rovers boss Darrell Clarke made four changes to his starting lineup following the weekend's exit from the FA Cup. Ellis Harrison and Tom Lockyer were away on international duty with the Welsh U-21

Southend United: Bentley, White, Barrett, Thompson, Coker, Hurst, Leonard, Atkinson, Worrall, Mooney (Pigott, 82), Payne
Substitutes: Prosser, Smith, O'Neill, Williams

Bristol Rovers: Nicholls, Clarke (J), Parkes, McChrystal, Brown, Bodin, Lines, Sinclair, Gosling (Montano, 56), Easter (Lucas, 72), Taylor
Substitutes: Mildenhall, Clarke, (O), Kilgour

squad, while Lee Mansell was rested and Daniel Leadbitter was injured.

That all meant starting places for Tom Parkes, Jermaine Easter, Chris Lines and James Clarke.

Apparently still angry after his side's FA Cup defeat at the hands of Scunthorpe, Southend boss Phil Brown made eight changes to his lineup and, almost as though they had a point to prove, his players were out of the blocks quickly.

They were ahead after 11 minutes, John White ghosting into the area and being allowed time and space to head past Lee Nicholls and their high tempo game caused Rovers a few problems in the opening stages.

In fact it took Rovers all of 30 minutes to get into their stride but when they did Billy Bodin's cracking effort was chalked off for an offside decision against Matty Taylor.

The second half belonged to Clarke's side who played some delightful football but just couldn't conjure up a goal. Twice Easter was thwarted by highly rated goalkeeper Daniel Bentley, who made a couple of other crucial saves to preserve his side's lead, leaving Rovers to concentrate on the league!

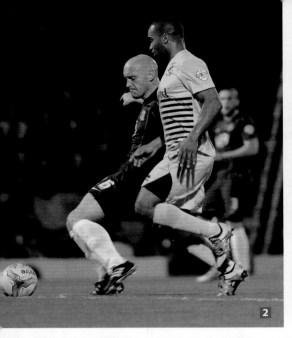

1. Rovers players take a look at the Roots Hall pitch

2. Jermaine Easter takes on former Rovers defender Adam Barrett

3. Some of the 181 Rovers supporters who made the Tuesday night trip to Roots Hall

4. Stuart Sinclair prepares to make his challenge

5. Billy Bodin keeps a close eye on the ball

6. Jamie Lucas feels the full force of this Adam Barrett challenge

7. Mark McChrystal wins this aerial battle

■ ■ ■ The Memorial Stadium – Saturday 14th November 2015 ■ ■ ■

Bristol Rovers **2-0** Carlisle United

Goals: Taylor (66 & 88)

Referee: Mark Brown
Attendance: 6,423

This was the 33rd league meeting between Rovers and Carlisle and honours were fairly even with Rovers having won 13 of the previous 32 encounters, Carlisle 11, with eight games being all square.

In charge of The Cumbrians was former Rovers player Keith Curle, who was celebrating his 52nd birthday and one of his charges was another former Rovers player, Angelo Balanta who was with the club during our one year sojourn in The Conference.

If I'm honest I don't recall too many memorable games against Carlisle, thought the one that does stand out, if only for the result, is a 2-0 win at Brunton Park back in August 2003 when Rovers' goals were scored by Wayne Carlisle!

Brunton Park was also the scene of the first away win under the stewardship of Paul Trollope following the sacking of Ian Atkins, back in October 2005.

Rovers were going through a somewhat barren spell in terms of results at The Mem, having won just one league game on their own patch all season, and that was against Barnet back in August.

If home results had matched those achieved on the road, then Darrell Clarke's side would surely be sitting pretty at the top of the league!

Clarke made just one change to his starting lineup, bringing in Cristian Montano for only his second league start of the campaign. In making that one change the manager probably made a little piece of history, as I certainly can't recall two League Two sides each having

 Bristol Rovers: Nicholls, Clarke (J), Parkes, McChrystal, Brown, Bodin, Sinclair, Lines (Clarke (O), 90), Montano (Gosling, 84), Easter (Blissett, 88), Taylor
Substitutes: Mildenhall, Mansell, Lucas, Kilgour

Carlisle United: Gillespie, Miller, Atkinson, Brough, Sweeney, Dicker, Balanta (Rigg, 61), Thompson (Ibehre, 61), Asamoah, Ellis, McQueen (Wyke, 79)
Substitutes: Hery, Hanford, Osei, Archibald-Henville

a Columbian in their starting XI. What's more, Montano and Balanta have both played for Rovers!

Enough of the trivia, though, and on to matters on the pitch where Rovers were out of the blocks quickly and might have opened their account as early as the fourth minute but Matty Taylor was denied by Mark Gillespie's fine save.

The keeper was in action again shortly afterwards, this time saving well from Jermaine Easter.

In spite of all of their first half possession though, Rovers were unable to make the breakthrough and it was possible to sense a degree of tension around the ground as home fans, desperate to see a home win, recalled previous games where Clarke's side had dominated only to lose following an opposition counter attack.

They needn't have worried, though, as Taylor scored at the end of a flowing move on 66 minutes. The collective sigh of relief that travelled around the stands and terraces told its own story. There was no way that lead was going to be surrendered and Taylor made sure that it would be an afternoon to celebrate as he scored again two minutes from time.

1 A one minute's silence was observed before kick off in memory of the victims of the atrocities in Paris

2 Chris Lines and Luke Joyce tussle for possession

3 Matty Taylor opens the scoring

4 There were a lot of photographers at this game!

5 Cristian Montano takes on Anthony Sweeney

6 Billy Bodin wins a header

7 Jermaine Easter gains possession

■ ■ **The Checkatrade.com Stadium – Saturday 21st November 2015** ■ ■

Crawley Town **2-1** Bristol Rovers

Goals: Murphy (10 & 11)

Referee: Trevor Kettle
Attendance: 2,612

Goal: Taylor (pen, 87)

R overs travelled to the ridiculously named Checkatrade.com Stadium for the fourth time looking for a first league win against their opponents.

Paul Buckle's side were soundly thrashed by four goals to one back in September 2011 in a game that summed up his reign. Reluctant to speak to the press afterwards, he had been petulant when reminded he was obliged to, and he also prevented any players from doing so!

Following his departure, in January 2012, the sides played out a goalless draw in that season's return fixture and next met in the FA Cup. Another goalless draw at The Mem meant a replay at the aforementioned stadium, on 18th December 2013, but that was abandoned after 74 minutes due to atrocious weather conditions.

The replay took place at the second time of asking, on the date of the third round of the competition, and Rovers ran out 2-1 winners thus earning the right to meet Birmingham.

A familiar face in the Crawley side was former Rovers striker Matt Harrold whose services were dispensed with following our drop into non league football.

Rovers boss Darrell Clarke was looking for his side to register a seventh away win of the season and equal a long standing club record of five consecutive away league wins.

He named an unchanged side for this match but couldn't have envisaged how slowly his charges would be out of the blocks.

They were two goals down after only 11 minutes, conceding twice to home striker Rhys Murphy. The first came after failure to

Crawley Town: Flavahan, Young, Yorwerth, Bradley, Hancox, Edwards (Ashton, 87), Smith, Walton, Deacon, Harrold (Rooney, 70), Murphy (Barnard, 84)
Substitutes: Scales, Preston, Fenelon, Jenkins

Bristol Rovers: Nicholls, Clarke (J) (Gosling, 76), Parkes, McChrystal (Lockyer, 46), Brown, Bodin, Lines, Sinclair Montano (Harrison), Easter, Taylor
Substitutes: Mildenhall, Leadbitter, Mansell, Clarke (O)

cut out a cross into the box which evaded everyone, hit Crawley's Roarie Deacon on the shin and rebounded into the path of Murphy who scored from close range.

A minute later the same player was allowed time and space to send a dipping, swerving, shot past Lee Nicholls and after that the home side seemed happy to defend in depth.

Clarke's side huffed and puffed but were unable to make a first half breakthrough even though Matty Taylor and Billy Bodin went close.

It was a similar story after the break as Crawley played with one player up front and Rovers gradually went from three to two at the back.

Bodin saw a shot hit the post and rebound into the arms of a grateful Darryl Flavahan before he was bundled over in the box with three minutes to go, allowing Taylor to register his ninth goal of the season from the penalty spot.

Possession, of which Rovers had 57%, counts for nothing though and Clarke's side were unable to get back on level terms and suffered only their second away league defeat of the season.

1 Thumbs up from these Gasheads at Crawley

2 Smiles before kick off!

3 Billy Bodin takes on Mitch Hancox

4 Tom Parkes faces Gwion Edwards

5 Matty Taylor scores a late consolation goal from the penalty spot

6 Jake Gosling closes down Lewis Young

7 Ellis Harrison challenges Luke Rooney

Bristol Rovers **1-2** Stevenage

Goal: Taylor (34)

Referee: Graham Salisbury
Attendance: 5,819

Goals: Schumacher (4), Whelpdale (60)

The only time these sides had played each other before was in a pre-season friendly in August 1998 when a 3-3 draw saw Barry Hayles, who had signed for Rovers from Stevenage a year earlier, scored twice against his former club.

The attraction, if indeed there was one, of this fixture was that Teddy Sheringham was the Stevenage manager. The former England international, holder of 51 caps was in his first season of club management.

The visitors had yet to win on their travels this season and arrived with a reputation for playing a long ball game, so Rovers supporters felt that it was a good opportunity to build on the win achieved against Carlisle in our previous home game.

Home results certainly needed to improve as two wins out of eight told its own story and the natives were, to coin a phrase, beginning to get restless!

Darrell Clarke made just two changes to his starting lineup and handed a debut to his latest signing, Paris Cowan-Hall, here on a moth's loan from Millwall.

Having conceded two early goals in their

previous game, at Crawley, Clarke must have been praying that his side didn't do the same on their own turf.

However his prayers went unanswered as they were behind with just four minutes on the clock when Steven Schumacher picked up on a poor Stuart Sinclair clearance and belted a shot into the net beyond the despairing dive of Lee Nicholls.

Bristol Rovers: Nicholls, Clarke (J) (Leadbitter, 78), Parkes, Lockyer, Brown, Bodin, Lines, Sinclair, Cowan-Hall (Montano, 66), Easter (Harrison, 66), Taylor
Substitutes: Mildenhall, McChrystal, Mansell, Clarke (O)

Stevenage: Day, Henry, Franks, Wells, Ogilvie, Pett, Tonge, Schumacher (Gorman, 90), Whelpdale (Gnanduillet, 90), Matt, Kennedy (Lee, 72)
Substitutes: McCombe, Hughes, Voss, Conlon

It took Clarke's side a while to recover from that blow, but recover they did and Cowan-Hall set up Matty Taylor for a shot with a delightful chip. The diminutive striker timed his run to avoid straying into an offside position and gleefully knocked the ball past 40 year old goalkeeper Chris Day to register his tenth goal of the season.

This observer, in common with many amongst the lowest league crowd of the season (5,819), thought that was the signal for Rovers to go on and overturn a Stevenage side that looked distinctly ordinary, in spite of the fact that they held the ball up well and appeared to be content with a point.

It turns out they weren't, as Chris Whelpdale's goal on the hour mark stunned everyone in the ground, apart from the 101 Stevenage fans who had bothered to make the trek down to Bristol on a Tuesday night.

The atmosphere, and the game, was muted after that and the visitors comfortably held on to take home all three points.

1. A lot of empty seats as the teams come out of the tunnel!

2. Paris Cowan-Hall challenges Ron Henry

3. Tom Parkes wins this header in spite of almost losing his shirt!

4. Tom Lockyer heads clear

5. James Clarke and Chris Whelpdale in a race for possession

6. Matty Taylor celebrates his goal

7. It's pasty time!

Exeter City **1-1** Bristol Rovers

Goal: Reid (90)

Referee: Philip Gibbs
Attendance: 5,548

Goal: Sinclair (84)

The last time Rovers travelled down to Exeter for a league fixture was on the opening day of the 2013/14 season, when The Grecians ran out 2-1 winners.

A nice little touch on this season's visit could be found outside the turnstiles as Exeter had posted 'welcome back' messages following our one year stint in The Conference.

This was the 77th league meeting between the sides, with honours even, 25 wins apiece and 26 draws prior to kick off.

Many players have turned out in the blue of Rovers and the red of Exeter, though on this occasion only two could boast that they had appeared for Pirates and Grecians.

Rovers Jake Gosling was one of them, Exeter's Will Hoskins the other, though neither featured in this match as Gosling was left out of the Rovers travelling party of 20 and Hoskins was missing through injury.

This, we were told on arrival, will be the last season the teams will change in the bowels of the Stagecoach Stand and what a relief that will be as they are cramped to say the least!

The old wooden stand and the shallow terrace reserved for away fans behind one goal are to make way for more modern structures at the end of this season and the dressing rooms will be located on the opposite side of the pitch beneath the main grandstand.

Exeter boss Paul Tisdale arrived early, having travelled down by train, accompanied by a good many Rovers supporters and described the journey as 'lively'! Dressed from head to toe in his Ted Baker gear, he spent a long time chatting amicably with backroom staff on arrival and seemed genuinely pleased that we had returned to league football after just one season away. In fact, that was the prevailing theme behind the scenes, from Tisdale to Steve Perryman (Director of Football) to every member of staff.

As for the game, well Darrell Clarke made four changes to his starting lineup and opted for a 5-3-2 formation.

The latest Rovers recruit, on loan Cambridge striker Rory Gaffney, led the line and made an impressive debut as Clarke's side took the game to their hosts in the first half and battered them in the second.

All they had to show for their efforts, though, was Stuart Sinclair's 84th minute strike and they were denied all three points when Jamie Reid equalised with virtually the last kick of the game.

The football from Rovers was scintillating, the possession 52% in their favour, but the points were, unfairly, in the opinion of many, shared.

Exeter City: *Olejnik, Davies, Brown, Moore-Taylor, Woodman (Nichols 86), Wheeler, Noble (Holmes, 46), Harley, Nicholls, Morrison (Tillson, 58), Reid*
Substitutes: McCready, Hamon, Watkins, Grant

Bristol Rovers: *Nicholls, Leadbitter (Bodin, 72), Clarke (J), Parkes, Lockyer, Brown, Mansell, Clarke (O), Sinclair, Gaffney (Harrison, 78), Taylor (Easter, 78)*
Substitutes: Mildenhall, McChrystal, Lines

1 Rovers players warm up in front of the home fans

2 Goalscorer Stuart Sinclair takes on Alex Nicholls

3 Tom Lockyer has a quiet word with the ref!

4 Lee Mansell gets in a challenge during a light shower!

5 Rory Gaffney in action on his Rovers debut

6 Ollie Clarke takes on Clinton Morrison

7 Bovril...a proper football drink!

■ ■ ■ The Memorial Stadium – Tuesday 1st December 2015 ■ ■ ■

Bristol Rovers 3-0 Wycombe Wanderers

Goals: Taylor (60, 62, 72)

Referee: Brendan Malone
Attendance: 6,136

For the second time this season Wycombe Wanderers were the visitors to The Memorial Stadium and were looking to avenge their defeat in the Johnstone's Paint Trophy back in October.

There is, of course, a little bit of history between the sides and has been ever since a game was called off, on the advice of Wycombe's Health and Safety Officer at the time, because of a thunderstorm. Rovers were leading at the time the match was abandoned and lost the re match.

Then, of course, Rovers beat The Chairboys at Adams Park on the penultimate day of the 2013/14 season, leaving them needing a point to avoid the drop into The Conference.

Had they achieved that, instead of losing their last day fixture against Mansfield, then either Wycombe or Northampton would have gone down.

Rovers' boss Darrell Clarke named an unchanged side for the match following his side's impressive showing down at Exeter, though his starting lineup did show five changes to the one that dumped the visitors out of the JPT.

As for Wycombe their boss Gareth Ainsworth named a side that showed six changes to the one beaten in October.

A fairly even first half saw one chance apiece, with Matt Ingram, the Wycombe shot stopper, touching a fierce drive from Ollie Clarke over the bar in the second minute while at the other end Sam Wood's 15th minute effort hit the post and rebounded behind for a goal kick.

Bristol Rovers: Nicholls, Leadbitter (Cowan-Hall, 79), Clarke (J), Parkes, Lockyer, Brown, Sinclair, Mansell, Clarke (O) (Bodin, 58), Taylor (Easter, 83), Gaffney
Substitutes: Mildenhall, McChrystal, Harrison, Montano

Wycombe Wanderers: Ingram, McCarthy, Rowe, Stewart, Jombati, Harriman, O'Nien, Bloomfield, Wood (Sellers, 71), Thomson (Ugwu, 67), Hayes (Holloway, 67)
Substitutes: McGinn, Banton, Kretzschmar, Lynch

It looked for all the world that one goal would determine the outcome, but Rovers striker Matty Taylor had other ideas.

Just on the hour mark, a cleverly worked free kick routine some 20 yards from goal saw Taylor strike a shot that left Ingram clutching at thin air before the ball nestled in the back of the net.

Two minutes later the striker was at it again. Another free kick, this time taken quickly by Stuart Sinclair, found Taylor in space and he once again beat Ingram to double his side's lead.

Another two minutes elapsed before he was denied a quick fire hat trick by Ingram who made a superb save from his powerful downward header.

The hat trick did arrive, though, on 72 minutes when Taylor took advantage of some hesitation by the visiting defenders in the penalty area, spun and volleyed a shot past Ingram.

It was the first Football League hat trick by a Rovers player since April 2012, when Eliot Richards scored a treble against Burton Albion, and put Clarke's side within two points of a play off place.

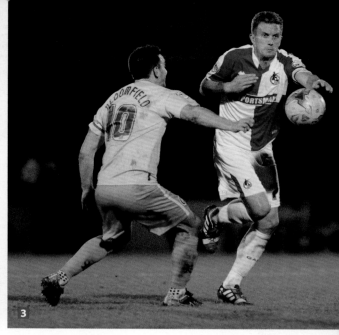

1 Matty Taylor and his team mates celebrate his hat trick
2 Rory Gaffney gets a shot away
3 Lee Mansell takes on Matt Bloomfield
4 Billy Bodin sidesteps a challenge by Danny Rowe
5 Up the Gas!
6 Daniel Leadbitter heads clear
7 Paris Cowan-Hall is confronted by Ryan Sellers

■ ■ ■ The Memorial Stadium – Saturday 12th December 2015 ■ ■ ■

Bristol Rovers 2-1 York City

Goals: Easter (71), Taylor (90)

Referee: Ben Toner
Attendance: 6,916

Goal: Oliver (41)

Rovers faced a home game against York City who had endured a pretty traumatic time since Jackie McNamara had taken over as manager following the sacking of Russ Wilcox.

York arrived in Bristol having equalled an unwanted club record of eight consecutive defeats, the last six of which had been under the stewardship of the new boss. It was a record the former Scotland and Celtic defender was keen to end.

Rovers, therefore, were expected to move into a top seven place with a comprehensive win.

The sides were meeting for the 44th time in the league and older supporters will, no doubt, recall the promotion season of 1973/74 when Rovers and The Minstermen were promoted to what is now The Championship along with Oldham Athletic.

Then, in 2004, both sides were trying to steer clear of the one relegation place when York arrived at The Mem in March 2004 in what for Rovers was the beginning of the Ian Atkins era. Rovers won and ended up climbing well clear of relegation, but York fell through the trap door and

into non-league football and here they are once more attempting to pull away from the lower reaches of League Two.

Just two years ago the sides met on four occasions, Rovers winning a league encounter 3-2 right at the beginning of the 2013/14 campaign and drawing the return fixture 0-0 in January. There had also been two more fixtures in the FA Cup, a 3-3 draw at The Mem being followed by a 3-2 win for John Ward's side in the replay at Bootham Crescent.

Bristol Rovers: *Nicholls, Clarke (J) (Leadbitter, 54), Parkes, Lockyer, Brown, Bodin (Easter, 70), Sinclair, Mansell, Cowan-Hall (Gosling, 54), Gaffney, Taylor*
Substitutes: Mildenhall, McChrystal, Clarke (O), Harrison

York City: *Flinders, O'Connor, Winfield, Boyle, Ilesanmi, McEvoy (Straker, 56), Penn, Summerfield (Godfrey, 88), Bennet, Fewster (Galbraith, 69), Oliver*
Substitutes: Carson, Swan, Ingham, Kitching

Rovers boss Darrell Clarke made two changes to his starting lineup for this game, recalling Billy Bodin and Paris Cowan-Hall in place of Daniel Leadbitter and Ollie Clarke, while Jake Gosling returned to the bench in place of Cristian Montano.

It was to be the last time we would see Cowan-Hall and Lee Nicholls in action for Rovers as both loanees were shortly to return to their parent clubs.

Nicholls conceded in the 41st minute when the unmarked Vadaine Oliver volleyed a close range effort past him. It was a lead they held until the 77th minute when substitute Jermaine Easter equalised with his first touch of the game, taking advantage of a Lee Mansell shot being deflected into his path and comfortably beating Scott Flinders.

With the game about to enter stoppage time, Matty Taylor conjured up a winner when he took a ball into the box from Jake Gosling on his chest and fired home from close range.

Tough for York, great for Rovers!

1. An unusual view of the players emerging from the tunnel
2. While Jermaine Easter almost loses his shirt, Matty Taylor nips in. Seconds later the ball was in the net
3. Hoping for a win
4. James Clarke beats Bradley Fewster to the ball

5. Jake Gosling gets a shot away
6. Billy Bodin closes in on Luke Summerfield
7. Rory Gaffney evades this challenge by Dave Winfield
8. Matty Taylor isn't best pleased with Russell Penn...the referee isn't best pleased with him!

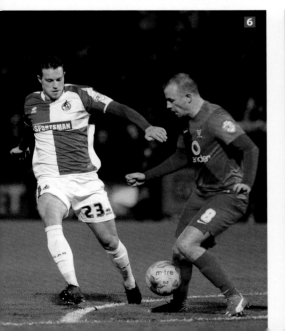

■ Chigwell Construction Stadium – Saturday 19th December 2015 ■

Dagenham & Redbridge 0-3 Bristol Rovers

Referee: Charles Breakspear
Attendance: 1,820

Goals: Brown (33), Gaffney (33), Bodin (90)

All the talk, amongst the assembled media hacks at what is now known as Chigwell Construction Stadium (whatever happened to good old Victoria Road?), was of the manager.

Wayne Burnett's side had not won a home game in the league all season and the pressure was on, in spite of a midweek FA Cup second round replay victory at non league Whitehawk.

To compound matters John Still, a former Rovers assistant manager and a man who enjoyed success as Dagenham manager, had been sacked by Luton three days before and was, allegedly, going to be at the game.

There were, in fact, two rumours doing the rounds in the press box. One was that The Daggers couldn't afford to pay Burnett off, the other that this would be his last game in charge.

This was the ninth league meeting between the sides though they did meet back in the LDV Vans Trophy back in 2001 when The Daggers were a non league side.

There have been some memorable encounters in the past and the hat trick that Jeff Hughes scored back in 2010 to give Rovers a 3-0 win was a particular highlight. Victoria Road, or whatever it's called, was also the ground on which Mitch Harding and Conor Gough made their Rovers debuts in the final game of the 2011/12 season, though we did get stuffed 4-0 on that occasion.

The following season French striker Oumare Tounkara scored the only goals of his Rovers career on the same ground as Rovers registered a 4-2 win. Gough also

Dagenham & Redbridge:
Cousins, Hoyte, Dikamona, Obileye (Nosworthy, 46), Connors, Passley, Labadie, Boucaud, Jones (Vassell, 65), Chambers, Doidge (Cureton, 65)
Substitutes: O'Brien, Raymond, Hemmings, Ferdinand

Bristol Rovers:
Puddy (Mildenhall, 49), Leadbitter (Bodin, 67), Clarke (J), Parkes, Lockyer, Brown, Sinclair (Gosling, 49), Clarke (O), Mansell, Gaffney, Taylor
Substitutes: McChrystal, Harrison, Easter, Cowan-Hall

played in that game, the second of his Rovers career and the last of his only two league appearances.

Gough replaced Steve Mildenhall on both occasions, so it was somewhat ironic that Mildenhall should again feature prominently in the latest match between the Pirates and The Daggers, arriving off the bench in the 49th minute to replace Will Puddy, who suffered a recurrence of the groin injury that had, up until this point, kept him out of action all season.

By that stage Rovers were ahead courtesy of Lee Brown's first half goal which came after a well worked free kick routine involving himself, Lee Mansell and Matty Taylor.

'Mildy' made one excellent save to preserve the lead and then watched as his colleagues stepped up a gear and scored twice in the closing stages through Rory Gaffney (his first for the club) and Billy Bodin to ensure Darrell Clarke's side occupied a play off spot going into the festive fixtures.

Oh, and there was no sign of Still at the game, but Burnett did get the sack two days later!

1 Rory Gaffney's first Gas Goal!

2 Billy Bodin scores goal number three

3 Ollie Clarke and Christian Doidge go head to head

4 Daniel Leadbitter beats Joss Labadie to the ball

5 James Clarke shadows Jodi Jones

6 It's Sheila, Uncle Jim and Derek!

7 Goal celebration for Lee Brown

■ The Cherry Red Records Stadium – Saturday 26th December 2015 ■

AFC Wimbledon **0-0** Bristol Rovers

Referee: Keith Hill
Attendance: 4,468

We were, if you recall, the first ever visitors to AFC Wimbledon on the occasion of their first ever match in the Football League back in 2011, when newly appointed boss Paul Buckle took his revamped Rovers side to Kingsmeadow (much better than The Cherry Red Records Stadium) for what was an historic occasion.

Nothing has really changed since that day some four years ago, but things are on the up for the club as they were recently (10th December) granted permission to develop the greyhound stadium in Plough Lane, Wimbledon.

Plans are now in place for a move to a new venue situated very close to their former ground. It is hoped that the 11,000 capacity stadium will be up and running for the start of the 2018/19 season.

Enough of the history lessons, though and moving swiftly on to this particular match that sold out on the day, causing a few problems for a number of Gasheads who had travelled without a ticket. Reports varied as to how many were unable to gain admission, from 30 to 100. It doesn't really matter what the final total was, though, as one is too many.

Team selection saw Darrell Clarke make five changes to the side that started against Dagenham & Redbridge seven days earlier, some enforced some not.

Steve Mildenhall continued in goal as Will Puddy's groin injury was still causing him problems, while Stuart Sinclair who also limped off against The Daggers missed out for the first time this season.

The home side, who hadn't won a game since a 2-0 victory against Hartlepool

AFC Wimbledon: *Shea, Fuller, Robinson, Osborne, Meades, Francomb, Bulman, Reeves, Barcham (Kennedy, 81), Taylor (Rigg, 81), Akinfenwa (Elliott, 72) Substitutes: Azeez, Fitzpatrick, Sweeney, McDonnell*

Bristol Rovers: *Mildenhall, Clarke (J) (Leadbitter, 46), Lockyer, McChrystal, Brown, Bodin, Clarke (O), Mansell, Gosling (Montano, 64), Harrison (Gaffney, 72), Taylor Substitutes: Parkes, Easter, Preston, Broom*

United on 31st October, and had been beaten by Forest Green Rovers in the FA Cup, were looking to get back to winning ways.

There was a one minute's applause in memory of Don Howe prior to kick off. The well respected coach had played his part in the success of the old Wimbledon side, working with manager Bobby Gould.

The match was barely four minutes old when AFC were reduced to ten men after Paul Robinson was red carded.

Ellis Harrison appeared to reach Matty Taylor's flick on ahead of the defender and went to ground under a hefty challenge. Robinson was the last line of the Dons defence and referee Keith Hill, having decided it was a foul, brandished a red card.

As far as drama went, that was it and while the ten men did enough to prevent Rovers making the breakthrough, Clarke's side were not at their best and given the paucity of goalscoring opportunities in the entire 90 minutes, a goalless draw was the inevitable outcome.

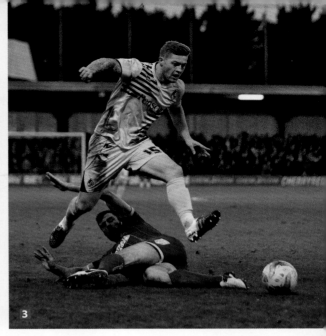

1. The calm before the storm!
2. Billy Bodin in a race with Dannie Bulman for the ball
3. James Clarke evades a challenge from Jonathan Meades
4. Matty Taylor hurdles over James Shea
5. Santa is a Gashead!
6. Ellis Harrison goes down under a challenge from Paul Robinson
7. Lee Brown gets past Jake Reeves

■ ■ ■ **The Memorial Stadium – Monday 28th December 2015** ■ ■ ■

Bristol Rovers **2-1** Leyton Orient

Goals: Gaffney (31 & 53)

Referee: Kevin Johnson
Attendance: 9,836

Goal: Simpson (45)

The second half of the season began with a visit from a Leyton Orient side who were tipped, in the summer, to gain automatic promotion.

When they beat Darrell Clarke's side back in August to seal a fifth consecutive win, you would have thought that they had already won the league. Their owners, wearing replica shirts under their expensively tailored suits, were high fiving everyone they met, and hugging the players and staff.

Fast forward to December and they arrived in Bristol below Rovers in the league table and looking to revive their bid for end of season honours.

Perhaps I'm being harsh, but I really didn't like the way they celebrated back then and was hoping that we would avenge that defeat in this, the 100th league meeting between the clubs.

Predictions beforehand were that we would attract a crown in excess of 8,500 but many fans were in the bars as soon as they opened, always a good sign that a bigger than average crowd is expected.

As it turned out, over 9,800 were inside the ground and were treated to an excellent

game of football by two well matched sides.

Prior to kick off striker Matty Taylor received the PFA November Player of the Month Award while finding himself out of the starting lineup as manager Darrell Clarke announced a side that saw six changes from the one that gained a point 48 hours earlier.

With Orient unbeaten in six games and Rovers in five, it was likely that something would give.

Bristol Rovers: *Mildenhall, Leadbitter, Parkes, Lockyer, Brown, Bodin (Clarke (J) 74), Mansell, Sinclair, Montano (Clarke, (O) 81), Easter (Taylor, 67), Gaffney Substitutes: McChrystal, Harrison, Gosling, Preston*

Leyton Orient: *Cisak, Clohessy, Essam, M'Voto (Shaw, 46), Kpekawa, Turgott, Pritchard, Payne, McAnuff (Kashket, 74), Simpson, Palmer (Marquis, 74) Substitutes: Dunne, Grainger, Moncur, Adeboyejo*

Clarke's side drew first blood when, just after the half hour mark, on loan striker Rory Gaffney slalomed through a static Orient defence before facing goalkeeper Alex Cisak and calmly giving the shot stopper no chance with his close range shot.

However League Two's top scorer, Jay Simpson, who had scored in the 45th minute of the August encounter between the sides, did it again in this match just when it seemed as though Rovers were in complete control.

Six minutes after the restart Gaffney topped his first half goal with a left foot volley that saw Cisak clutching thin air as he dived to his left, but there was no way he could prevent the striker claiming his third Rovers goal.

There were one or two anxious moments for Rovers but, by and large, they did more than enough to warrant victory and we might even have seen a Gaffney hat trick had it not been for Cisak who stopped one of the striker's efforts with his legs and comfortably held on to a late header from the in form loanee.

■ TWO TO ONE ■

1 *Rory Gaffney opens the scoring*
2 *Ollie Clarke is fouled by Scott Kashket*
3 *Daniel Leadbitter is pushed off the ball by Jobi McAnuff*
4 *Cristian Montano closes in on Sean Clohessy*

5 *Matty Taylor in pursuit of Frazer Shaw*
6 *Stuart Sinclair wrong foots his marker*
7 *New scarves for Christmas?*

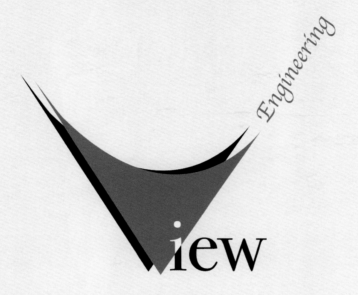

Proudly Supporting The Gas

Congratulations to all players and staff
for the amazing achievements
over the last two seasons

- ▼ HGV – Service, Inspection, MOT and Repairs
- ▼ Construction equipment – Service and Repair
- ▼ Marine Engineering – Engine Repairs
- ▼ Welding and Fabrication

Contact Wayne on - Office: 0117 9807281

Mobile: 07765 222820

Email: info@view-engineering.co.uk

■ ■ ■ The Memorial Stadium – Saturday 2nd January 2016 ■ ■ ■

Bristol Rovers **2-0** Luton Town

Goals: Gaffney (60 & 72)

Referee: Lee Swabey
Attendance: 9,131

Just five days after saying goodbye to 2015 at The Memorial Stadium, Rovers opened their 2016 programme of games at the same venue.

Another crowd in excess of 9,000 turned up for the visit of Luton Town and they weren't to be disappointed.

Rovers, thanks to one of Luton's old boys, Stuart Sinclair, had beaten The Hatters at Kenilworth Road in August and were looking for their first double of the season and, indeed, their first since the 2012/13 campaign.

Luton had dispensed with the services of former Rovers assistant manager John Still just before Christmas and arrived in Bristol with their Head of Academy, Andy Awford in temporary charge. He had 'previous' against Rovers as he was in charge at Portsmouth when Rovers were beaten 3-2 at Fratton Park back in April 2014.

Rovers boss Darrell Clarke again made changes to his starting lineup, though on this occasion there were only three after the five and six, respectively, made for the games against AFC Wimbledon and Leyton Orient.

Those changes saw Ollie Clarke, James Clarke and Matty Taylor return in place of Billy Bodin, Cristian Montano and Jermaine Easter.

Awford made two changes to his side as he looked to kickstart their season and for the second time this season Luton didn't register an on target shot against Rovers which is quite a remarkable stat from 180 minutes of football.

Rovers, looking to extend their unbeaten run and aiming to record a fifth consecutive win on home soil, probably

Bristol Rovers: Mildenhall, Leadbitter, Clarke (J), Lockyer, Parkes, Brown, Sinclair, Clarke (O), Mansell, Gaffney (Harrison, 90), Taylor (Easter, 87)
Substitutes: McChrystal, Lines, Montano, Preston, Bodin

Luton Town: Tyler, O'Donnell, Cuthbert, Okuonghae, Howells (McCourt, 69), McGeechan, Lawless, Smith, Hall, Mackail-Smith (Marriott, 82), Benson (McQuoid, 72)
Substitutes: Justham, Lee, Long, Wilkinson

had the better of the first half exchanges, though their goalbound efforts were either wide of the target or blocked by a Luton side seemingly intent on leaving Bristol with at least a point.

The best opportunity of the half saw Lee Mansell denied a goal by Mark Tyler's fingertip save five minutes before the half time interval and it was to be the hour mark before the first goal arrived.

By that time the visitors had seen Cameron McGeehan hit a shot over the bar and Ryan Hall fire another effort into the side netting.

Rory Gaffney, though, pounced after a Tom Lockyer header had been cleared off the line and lashed the ball high into the Luton net.

12 minutes later it was game over as the striker, playing the final game of his loan spell, scored his second goal. After Tyler spilt his first effort, he simply knocked the ball back past the unfortunate keeper with his second. It was the second time in a week that the 'Ginger Messi' had scored a double and he had, no doubt, increased his value in the transfer market.

1 James Clarke, Tom Parkes, Lee Brown and Tom Lockyer applaud Gasheads at the end of the game

2 Jermaine Easter shields the ball from goalkeeper Mark Tyler

3 Lee Brown congratulates Steve Mildenhall on keeping a clean sheet

4 Daniel Leadbitter takes on Ryan Hall

5 Rory Gaffney, who scored a double for the second time in six days

6 Matty Taylor gets a shot away

7 Tell me they aren't texting each other!

■ ■ ■ **The Hive – Saturday 9th January 2016** ■ ■ ■

Barnet **1-0** Bristol Rovers

Goals: Hoyte (5)

Referee: Michael Bull
Attendance: 2,770

Our second visit to The Hive, Barnet's relatively new ground, still didn't convince me that this was the type of ground I would want the team I support to play in.

To be honest, if it's anything like Barnet's then I would rather we stayed at The Memorial Stadium.

The Hive, whilst functional, appears to lack character. I'm sure it suits Barnet's needs and that they have scope to generate a steady income stream from hiring out the surrounding pitches, both grass and artificial.

Rovers headed to North London looking to complete a double over last season's Conference rivals, having beaten Martin Allen's side 3-1 when they visited The Memorial Stadium last August.

With seven games unbeaten behind them Darrell Clarke's side were looking to extend their impressive run, but would have to make do without the services of Rory Gaffney, who had signed off his loan spell from Cambridge with two goals against Luton Town.

The popular striker had let everyone know that he would prefer to remain with Rovers, but instead found himself lining up for The U's in their game against Crawley as Rovers kicked off at The Hive.

His absence was the only change to the side, Ellis Harrison stepping up to the plate; yet another chance for the talented, but erratic, striker.

The day couldn't have turned out worse for both parties as Gaffney's side were beaten 1-0 at Crawley where another former Rovers striker, Matt Harrold, scored the only goal of the game and Rovers went down by the same score.

Barnet: *Stephens, Hoyte, Johnson, Dembele, N'Gala, Yiadom, Togwell, Weston, Gambin, Akinde, (Batt 81), McLean (Champion, 65)*
Substitutes: Gash, Stevens, Odoffin, McKenzie-Lyle, Taylor

Bristol Rovers: *Mildenhall, Leadbitter, Clarke (J), (Easter, 64), Lockyer, Parkes, Brown, Sinclair, Clarke (O) (Lines, 46), Mansell (Lawrence, 64), Harrison, Taylor*
Substitutes: McChrystal, Montano, Preston, Bodin

Clarke's side made the worst possible start, as the home side were quickly out of the blocks and began launching balls into the Rovers area, mostly from long throw ins.

It was their failure to clear a fifth minute missile that led to the goal, Gavin Hoyte lashing the ball high into the net from seven yards.

From then on Rovers dominated proceedings and Harrison wasted two good opportunities to equalise before the break. It was the same in the second half, even more so following the dismissal of home skipper Andy Yiadom for a foul on Stuart Sinclair just after the hour mark.

Barnet simply retreated back to the edge of their own area, meaning Rovers had the freedom to do what they wanted with the ball in the rest of the pitch.

Substitute Liam Lawrence, signed in the week from Shrewsbury, was unlucky to see a shot just clear the bar, while a shot from Sinclair landed on top of the net.

However they were unable to unlock the well organised home defence and they and over 1,200 Gasheads returned home empty handed.

1 Train passengers get a glimpse of what's happening at The Hive

2 Lee Brown is tackled by Andy Yiadom

3 Ellis Harrison and Bira Dembele tussle for possession

4 Ollie Clarke on the ball as two Barnet defenders close in

5 Tom Parkes tackles former Rovers striker John Akinde

6 Liam Lawrence, pictured on his Rovers debut

7 Is the programme as good as The Pirate?

■ ■ ■ The Kassam Stadium – Sunday 17th January 2016 ■ ■ ■

Oxford United **1-2** Bristol Rovers

Goal: Roofe (47)

Referee: Nick Kinseley
Attendance: 9,492

Goals: Taylor (53), Harrison (penalty, 88)

Looking to bounce back from defeat against Barnet, Rovers travelled to The Kassam Stadium where they had recorded victories in their two previous visits.

The home side had beaten Premiership side Swansea City in the FA Cup and Millwall in the Area Final of the Johnstone's Paint Trophy in the week leading up to this game.

In the seven days between this match and the trip to The Hive, manager Darrell Clarke had brought Rory Gaffney back to the club on a permanent basis, the club having agreed to pay Cambridge United an undisclosed fee to bring 'The Ginger Messi' back to The Mem.

Down the years there have been many players who have worn the colours of both clubs and there were three with Oxford connections in the Rovers starting lineup on this occasion, namely Lee Mansell, James Clarke and Matty Taylor.

The aforementioned Gaffney was one of two changes to the starting lineup for this game. He replaced Ellis Harrison while Chris Lines came in for Ollie Clarke.

The manager had warned his players beforehand that Oxford liked to retain possession as much as possible and that proved to be the case in the opening 45 minutes of a goalless, but absorbing, contest.

The complexion of the game changed immediately after the break as Oxford took a short corner and Rovers defenders momentarily switched off. The ball was driven low into the box where it bobbled around for what seemed like an eternity before dropping at the feet of Oxford's leading goalscorer Kemar Roofe who

Oxford United: Slocombe, Baldock, Mullins, Wright, Skarz, Roofe, Sercombe, Lundstarm, MacDonald (Hylton, 79), Taylor (O'Dowda, 33), Maguire (Hoban, 79)
Substitutes: Buchel, Ruffels, Dunkley, Evans

Bristol Rovers: Mildenhall, Leadbitter, Clarke (J), Parkes, Lockyer, Brown, Sinclair, Mansell (Clarke (O) 69), Lines, Gaffney (Harrison, 85), Taylor (Easter, 76)
Substitutes: McChrystal, Montano, Preston, Bodin

didn't pass up the opportunity of putting his side ahead within 50 seconds of the restart.

Six minutes later Rovers equalised following Daniel Leadbitter's run and cross to the near post where Taylor gleefully headed the ball past goalkeeper Sam Slocombe. The former Oxford man could have added a second but blazed the ball over the bar when played in by Gaffney.

It might have been a costly miss as home substitute Callum O'Dowda looked to have beaten Steve Mildenhall with a shot that seemed destined for the top corner. However the keeper launched himself to his left before touching the effort just over the bar.

A swift Rovers counter attack two minutes from time resulted in Slocombe dashing off his line and bringing down Jermaine Easter for what was a clear cut penalty, despatched with some aplomb by Ellis Harrison who, unbeknown to the 2,359 travelling Gasheads, would be driving straight up to Hartlepool after the match having agreed a one month loan deal with the Monkey Hangers.

1 Warming up at
The Kassam

2 James Clarke
tackles
Jake Wright

3 Up the Gas!

4 Chris Lines
closes in on
Chris Maguire

5 Matty Taylor
equalises

6 Ellis Harrison
celebrates his late
winner from the
penalty spot

7 Matty Taylor and
Rory Gaffney
celebrate at the
final whistle

■ ■ ■ The Memorial Stadium – Saturday 23rd January 2016 ■ ■ ■

Bristol Rovers **1-1** Plymouth Argyle

Goal: Bodin (79)

Referee: Oliver Langford
Attendance: 10,190

Goal: Simpson (88)

The 86th league meeting between these two clubs promised to be a cracking game with Argyle heading the League Two table and Rovers in fourth place nine points behind their long time Devon rivals.

The season's earlier encounter, down at Home Park back in September had ended all square, thanks to goals in the final five minutes from Argyle's Jake Jervis whose strike was cancelled out by Ellis Harrison's late penalty.

The game at The Mem was an all ticket affair and the visitors sold out of their allocation long before the day of the game. A late flurry of activity from Rovers fans, who had until midnight on the day before the game to purchase tickets meant that there would be a crowd in excess of 10,000.

The eagerly awaited clash saw two former Rovers players in the starting lineup for The Greens, namely Ryan Brunt and Gary Sawyer, while former Argyle player Jermaine Easter was on the bench for The Gas.

This was one of the rare occasions that manager Darrell Clarke was able to name an unchanged starting lineup. In fact his only change came on the bench where Ellis Harrison was absent following his loan move to Hartlepool and he was replaced by Ryan Broom who had played well against Mangotsfield United in the week.

It was the start of what could be a momentous week for Rovers as their ongoing legal dispute with Sainsbury's came to a head, though the outcome of the three day hearing would not be known until March.

Bristol Rovers: Mildenhall, Leadbitter, Clarke (J) (Bodin, 55), Parkes, Lockyer, Brown, Sinclair, Mansell (Montano, 55), Lines, Gaffney, Taylor (Easter, 76)
Substitutes: McChrystal, Clarke (O), Preston, Broom

Plymouth Argyle: McCormick, Mellow, Nelson, Hartley, Sawyer, Jervis (Threlkeld, 89), McHugh, Simpson, Wylde (Carey, 90), Brunt, Reid (Tanner, 61)
Substitutes: Harvey, Purrington, Bittner, Forster

First things first, though, and the most pressing item on the agenda was three points against the league leaders.

First half opportunities were few and far between, though Matty Taylor did see a long range effort comfortably held by Argyle goalkeeper Luke McCormick while Steve Mildenhall somehow got a touch on a piledriver from Argyle's Gregg Wylde and pushed it on to the crossbar.

Argyle and their boss felt they controlled the first half, while I have to be honest and say that I felt it was a very even 45 minutes.

Things changed after the break as the visitors enjoyed a brief period of dominance before Clarke rang the changes with a double substitution, followed by a third with 14 minutes of the game remaining.

Even before that, Rovers were the team in the ascendancy, and eventually all three subs combined to open the scoring on 79 minutes.

Billy Bodin got the final touch, his fifth goal of the season, and Rovers looked set for victory until two minutes from time when Josh Simpson rifled a shot past Mildenhall.

1 Celebrating Billy Bodin's goal

2 Rory Gaffney is stopped in his tracks by Gary Sawyer

3 Matty Taylor's effort is saved by Luke McCormick

4 Tom Parkes takes on Kelvin Mellor

5 Billy Bodin's goal

6 Cristian Montano tackles Oscar Threlkeld

7 Bad hair day, boys?

Accrington Stanley **1-0** Bristol Rovers

Goal: McConville (70)

Referee: Mark Haywood
Attendance: 2,027

Rovers headed north the day before the match hoping to register their first ever win at what is now known as The Wham Stadium.

The evening at the team hotel saw three players making their first overnight trip, namely Rory Gaffney, Liam Lawrence and Rory Fallon, stick to the tradition of undertaking their initiation ceremony.

The custom usually involves singing (badly!). Messrs Gaffney and Lawrence didn't disappoint and duly wailed their way through a couple of unrecognisable songs before Fallon, the club's recent acquisition, on non contract terms, took to the stage.

The New Zealander wowed his team mates and, later that evening, several thousand viewers on YouTube, with his performance of the Haka, the traditional Maori ancestral war cry, thus putting his team mates in good spirits ahead of the match.

Connections between the two sides are few and far between, though Joe Jacobson, Adam Dawson and Aaron Chapman have all worn the red of Stanley and the blue and white of Rovers.

Manager Darrell Clarke made two changes to his starting lineup, one of them seeing Liam Lawrence come in for his first start in a Rovers shirt, the other saw Billy Bodin reinstated. These two replaced Daniel Leadbitter and Chris Lines.

Meanwhile Accrington boss John Coleman surprised everyone by handing rookie shot stopper Ross Etheridge his league debut.

In spite of the bitterly cold conditions Rovers had a following of 543 which represented a quarter of the total attendance of just over 2,000 but by close of play most of them, as they tried to thaw out, were probably wishing they hadn't made the trek.

Etheridge did well, just after the 20 minute mark, to touch behind a cross/shot from Rory Gaffney that seemed destined for the top corner, before the striker then directed a header wide from the subsequent corner. That was the best chance of the half for Clarke's side.

The closest the home side came to scoring came from Adam Buxton who saw his fierce 30 yard drive pushed away by Steve Mildenhall as far as Billy Kee whose tame effort was comfortably saved.

Lawrence was denied a goal when his angled drive was saved by Etheridge, while Mildenhall kept his side in the game when he made an instinctive save from Sean McConville's close range header. However the same player scored the game's only goal after 70 minutes with what, in all honesty, was a cross which deceived everyone including Mildenhall.

Clarke sent on the cavalry in the shape of Jermaine Easter, Cristian Montano and Rory Fallon, all to no avail as the massed Accrington ranks could not be breached.

 Accrington Stanley: *Etheridge, Halliday, Pearson, Wright, Buxton, Mingoia, Crooks, Conneely, McConville, McCartan, Kee Substitutes: Davies, Proctor, Gornell, Wakefield, Brown, Carver, Mooney*

 Bristol Rovers: *Mildenhall, Clarke (J), Parkes, Lockyer, Brown, Bodin, Mansell, Sinclair, Lawrence, (Montano, 76), Gaffney, (Fallon, 76), Taylor, (Easter, 76) Substitutes: Leadbitter, McChrystal, Lines, Preston*

1 The delights of The Wham Stadium, pictured from the away terrace

2 Rory Fallon, pictured on his Rovers debut

3 Lee Mansell is closed down by Seamus Conneely

4 Rovers fans kept singing in spite of the atrocious weather

5 Liam Lawrence prepares to shoot

6 Tom Parkes challenges Brad Halliday

7 Stuart Sinclair on the attack

1

■ ■ ■ Fratton Park – Saturday 13th February 2016 ■ ■ ■

Portsmouth **3-1** Bristol Rovers

Goals: Evans (19), Smith (45), McNulty (76)

Referee: Trevor Kettle
Attendance: 17,808

Goal: Brown (90)

Old fashioned and outdated it might be, but Fratton Park is a proper football ground and there is always a great atmosphere when almost full to capacity which, these days, is around 19,000.

Behind the scenes is a veritable rabbit warren of corridors and rooms used for hospitality, storage, dressing rooms and offices, with a separate media suite in one corner of the ground making it a long walk for the victorious manager after the game, and an even longer one for the man in charge of the losing XI!

Rovers certainly don't have a good record against Pompey, having lost 15 of their previous 29 encounters. In fact the last time they won at Fratton Park it was against Millwall, on April Fool's Day 1978. The London club had been banned from playing on their own turf due to trouble at The Den (there's a surprise!).

A number of players have turned out in the colours of both clubs; Phil Roberts and David Hillier spring to my mind, while one of Rovers' latest acquisitions, Liam Lawrence, spent two years with Pompey and was in the starting lineup for The Gas on this occasion.

An unbelievable number of Gasheads, 2,863, made the journey down to Portsmouth to see if their side could get things back on track following the disappointment of losing to Accrington two weeks before.

Heavy rain in the week leading up to the match made for a difficult surface, though whether or not that affected manager Darrell Clarke's team selection isn't known.

Portsmouth: Fulton, Davies, Burgess, Webster, Stevens, Close, Doyle, Evans, Roberts (McGurk, 74), Bennett (Chaplin, 86), Smith (McNulty, 68)
Substitutes: Barton, Tollitt, Clarke, Bass

Bristol Rovers: Mildenhall, Leadbitter, Parkes, Lockyer, Brown, Bodin, Mansell (Montano, 55), Sinclair, Lawrence (Lines, 76), Gaffney, Easter (Taylor, 55)
Substitutes: McChrystal, Clarke (O), Puddy, Fallon

Anyway, he made two changes to his starting lineup, bringing in Daniel Leadbitter and Jermaine Easter for James Clarke and Matty Taylor respectively. It was Easter's first start since 28th December.

As early as the second minute goalkeeper Steve Mildenhall made an outstanding save to deny Pompey a goal, getting down low to keep out a header from Christian Burgess. Undeterred, the home side continued to take the game to Clarke's side as they continued playing at a high tempo.

They took a 19th minute lead through Gareth Evans and although Rory Gaffney struck the crossbar five minutes later, it was one of the few times that Rovers threatened to score.

Michael Smith added a second goal deep into first half stoppage time and a third goal arrived on 76 minutes courtesy of substitute Marc McNulty.

Rovers kept plugging away, but were indebted to Mildenhall for keeping the score down to a respectable three and they did at least score a consolation goal in stoppage time when Lee Brown rifled a free kick past Ryan Fulton.

1 Warming up at Fratton Park

2 On the way to the match

3 Billy Bodin takes on Enda Stevens

4 Daniel Leadbitter tries to get round Kyle Bennett

5 Stuart Sinclair stretches to beat Gary Roberts to the ball

6 Darrell Clarke gets the ball back to Daniel Leadbitter

7 Rory Gaffney is foiled by Ryan Fulton

BRISTOL TRANSMISSIONS

The Driveline Specialist

1

■ ■ ■ NEW OWNERS FOR BRISTOL ROVERS ■ ■ ■

On 19th February 2016 it was announced that the club had been acquired by the eminent Jordanian Al Qadi family and that, as part of the deal, Mr Wael Al Qadi would become President of the club.

The former Chairman of Swansea City, Steve Hamer, became Chairman of Bristol Rovers with immediate effect, replacing former Chairman Nick Higgs.

Speaking about the takeover, Wael said; "I've been a passionate football fan all of my life and I am excited about becoming involved with Bristol Rovers, which has such an amazing heritage and loyal fan base.

"We really see the potential of this great club. Bristol Rovers has always been known as a family club and it is my family's wish to maintain that tradition, through our own involvement and commitment.

"Whilst we will be investing in the club, we also want to see the club grow organically and we will be introducing a good recruitment policy, new structure, and a new Academy system that will produce a flow of players into the first team. We believe in a mix of home grown youth and experience to achieve the success this club, and the region, deserves."

The former Board of Directors, with the exception of the Supporters Club representatives, all stood down and were made Vice Presidents of the club while outgoing Chairman, Nick Higgs, said; "I sincerely believe that Bristol Rovers can count itself as being very fortunate to attract the interest of the Al Qadi family. This club deserves to have considerably more prominence on the football map.

"The Board promised the supporters, on many occasions, that it would only agree to the sale of the club if the right person expressed a serious interest."

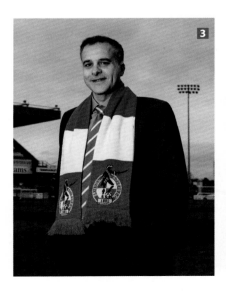

2

3

4

1 Speaking at the press conference to announce the new ownership of the club are Wael Al Qadi (centre) flanked by his brother Samer (right) and chairman Steve Hamer (left)

2 Wael takes questions from the assembled media representatives

3 Wael with his new attire!

4 Steve Hamer and Wael shake on it!

The day after the takeover, Wael attended his first game at The Memorial Stadium and he was seen at many more matches in the following weeks. The photos on this page were taken at some of them.

5 Morecambe - on the pitch with family members

6 Wycombe - in with the Rovers supporters

7 Exeter City - with Dutch Gas prior to kick off

8 Crawley Town - watching from Box One at The Mem

9 Carlisle United - with chairman Steve Hamer

10 Mansfield Town - in Box One and flying the flag!

Bristol Rovers **2-1** Morecambe

Goals: Gaffney (68), Bodin (78)

Referee: Darren England
Attendance: 7,400

Goal: Devitt (pen, 12)

Rovers' fans must have woken up wondering if they had been dreaming after the events of the previous day.

Friday 19th February turned out to be a truly momentous and historic day in the history of our football club, as it was taken over by the Jordanian Al Qadi family.

At a 1.30pm press conference the previous board members, led by Chairman Nick Higgs, formally stepped down and were replaced by the new owner and Club President, Wael Al Qadi and new Chairman Steve Hamer in front of the largest press gathering seen at The Mem in a long while.

The news was met, at first, by disbelief and it really did take a while to sink in, especially those of us caught up in the day's events.

It wasn't a dream, as we all discovered on matchday as there were a great many new faces in Box One for the match against Morecambe.

The directors who had stepped down had been made Vice Presidents of the club and it must have seemed a little bit surreal as they watched their successors introduced to the fans, on the balcony

of Box One before the game and on the pitch at half time.

As for the match, manager Darrell Clarke made three changes to his starting lineup, bringing in James Clarke, Chris Lines and Matty Taylor for Lee Mansell, Billy Bodin and Jermaine Easter.

The manager also named Tom Lockyer as skipper, the first time the young Welshman had taken the armband.

Bristol Rovers: *Mildenhall, Leadbitter, Clarke (J) (Bodin 32), Lockyer, Parkes, Brown, Sinclair, Lines (Clarke (O) 90), Lawrence, Taylor (Easter, 78), Gaffney*
Substitutes: McChrystal, Montano, Puddy, Fallon

Morecambe: *Roche, Deeley, Edwards, Dugdale (Kenyon, 36), Parrish, Devitt (Wildig, 75), Goodall, Fleming, Ellison, Barkhuizen, Mullin (Wilson, 65)*
Substitutes: Bondswell, Hedley, O'Hara

The sides had shared seven goals in this season's previous meeting, at The Globe Arena, Rovers eventually winning 4-3 and with Morecambe only able to name six substitutes for this game, there were high expectations of a convincing Rovers victory on this occasion.

Things seldom go according to plan, though, and this was one such occasion. Not helped by a swirling wind, both sides found it difficult to get the ball down and play and the only effort of any real note in the first half saw Morecambe take the lead from the penalty spot. Tom Parkes was adjudged to have handled and Jamie Devitt converted the spot kick.

Rovers stepped up a gear after the break and goals from Rory Gaffney and Billy Bodin ensured victory in front of the new owners.

Morecambe ended the match with ten men after Andy Fleming received a straight red card for pulling Stuart Sinclair's ponytail, in a game that will only be remembered as the start of a new era for the club, not for the free flowing football!

1 Thumbs up from new owner Wael Al Qadi
2 Lee Brown is challenged by Tom Barkhuizen
3 Liam Lawrence on the attack
4 Tom Lockyer is determined not to let Paul Mullin past

5 Goalscorers Billy Bodin and Rory Gaffney
6 Lee Brown on the ball
7 Wael meets two young Gasheads

■ ■ ■ Adams Park – Saturday 27th February 2016 ■ ■ ■

Wycombe Wanderers **1-0** Bristol Rovers

Goal: O'Nien (85)

Referee: C Sarginson
Attendance: 4,759

After a week when football seemed to take a back seat amongst the club's supporters, given the takeover seven days before, it was time to return to action against Wycombe Wanderers at Adams Park.

The new owners had been keen to play down the fact that Rovers are now a wealthy club and President Wael Al Qadi had gone out and said as much in an interview with King of the football journos, Henry Winter, in The Times.

What was quickly becoming obvious was that there is a willingness to build/restructure the club on a gradual basis and not just come in and throw money at it. The club will, in due course, see the infrastructure overhauled and the phrase 'evolution not revolution' turned out to be the most popular one of the week.

Over 1,000 Rovers supporters made the relatively short trip to Adams Park. In fact the 1,629 made it the fourth highest away following of the season.

Everyone, I'm sure, has their own special memories of Adams Park, the scene of a few controversial moments in recent times, but we have covered that in a previous match report already this season.

This was the third meeting between the clubs, with Rovers ahead on points, having won 2-0 in the Johnstone's Paint Trophy and 3-0 in the league in games played at The Mem before Christmas.

Darrell Clarke made four changes for this game, the players to lose out on this occasion being Matty Taylor, Tom Parkes, Stuart Sinclair and Chris Lines, and in their place came Jermaine Easter, Mark McChrystal, Ollie Clarke and Lee Mansell.

Wycombe Wanderers: *Allsop, O'Nien, Stewart, McCarthy, Jacobson, McGinn, Harriman, Bean (Wood, 21), Bloomfield, Hayes, Kretzschmar (Ugwu, 81) Substitutes: Jombati, Richardson, Sellers*

Bristol Rovers: *Mildenhall, Leadbitter (Bodin, 56), Clarke (J), Lockyer, McChrystal, Brown, Clarke (O), Mansell, Lawrence (Fallon, 87), Easter (Taylor, 67), Gaffney Substitutes: Parkes, Lines, Montano, Puddy*

For skipper McChrystal it was his first start of the year, his last appearance being against AFC Wimbledon on Boxing Day.

The opening 45 minutes were mostly forgettable, possibly because there was too much at stake, with the winner being guaranteed a top seven place at the end of the game.

The best chance of the half came in the last minute of the 45 and Matt Bloomfield really should have done better than blaze the ball over the top after finding himself with only Steve Mildenhall to beat.

Things did improve after the break and had Rovers been able to take advantage of one of their many set plays then perhaps they might have returned home with all three points.

However it was left to the home side to score the game's only goal with five minutes remaining, inevitably from a set play, Luke O'Nien heading past Mildenhall from Joe Jacobson's free kick as Rovers defenders seemed to switch off for the first and only time of the afternoon.

1. Pitch inspection at Adams Park
2. Come on Gas!
3. Lee Brown gets in a cross in spite of Matt Bloomfield's challenge
4. Ollie Clarke is thwarted by Matt Bloomfield
5. Tom Lockyer closes in on Max Kretzschmar

6. Mark McChrystal gets to the ball ahead of Paul Hayes
7. Lee Mansell tackles Stephen McGinn with back up from Jermaine Easter!
8. Rory Gaffney tangles with Michael Harriman

■ ■ ■ **The Memorial Stadium – Tuesday 1st March 2016** ■ ■ ■

Bristol Rovers **4-1** Hartlepool United

Goals: Taylor (10, 38, 56), Gaffney (31)

Referee: Lee Swabey
Attendance: 6,634

Goal: Paynter (52)

Whoever is in charge of the Football League fixtures computer needs to have another look at a programme that throws up a game between Bristol Rovers and Hartlepool United on a Tuesday night.

At least we made the trip up to the north east on a fairly mild evening last September, while Hartlepool had to make the reverse trip on a cold and windy February night.

Darrell Clarke, a former Hartlepool player, of course, saw his side register a comfortable 3-0 victory in the first encounter between the sides this season and was looking for more of the same following defeat at Wycombe.

The manager made three changes to his starting lineup, recalling Matty Taylor, Chris Lines and Billy Bodin at the expense of Jermaine Easter, Ollie Clarke and Daniel Leadbitter though he revealed, in his pre match interview, that midfielder Stuart Sinclair's groin injury could keep him out for six weeks.

Also included in Clarke's squad was Ellis Harrison, whose loan spell at Hartlepool

ended on 20th February but whose appearances for The Monkey Hangers were limited to three before he picked up an ankle injury.

Rovers might have taken a first minute lead had Taylor not headed over from a Lee Brown cross.

It mattered little, though, as the striker who had just one goal to his name from his previous 11 games, opened the scoring with ten minutes on the clock when his

---

Bristol Rovers: Mildenhall, Clarke (J), Lockyer, McChrystal, Brown, Bodin, Mansell (Clarke (O), 82), Lines, Lawrence, Taylor (Easter, 75), Gaffney (Harrison, 78)
Substitutes: Leadbitter, Parkes, Montano, Puddy

Hartlepool United: Carson, Magnay, Jackson, Harrison, Carroll, James, Gray, Featherstone (Hawkins, 66), Walker, Thomas (Fenwick, 59), Paynter (Oates, 82)
Substitutes: Richards, Laurent, Caig

---

left foot volley beat goalkeeper Trevor Carson.

Somewhere between that point and the 31st minute, when Rovers doubled their lead, play was halted because it was drawn to the referee's attention that Matthew Bates, listed as number six on the official teamsheet wasn't in fact, on the pitch but number five Scott Harrison was. Apparently the fourth official forgot to tell the referee that Bates had been injured in the warm up!

Anyway, Rory Gaffney walked the ball into the net for the second goal and Taylor headed his second of the night on 38 minutes while Brad Walker rattled the Rovers crossbar in first half stoppage time.

Billy Paynter's 52nd minute goal saw his goalkeeper celebrate as though they had won the match. His joy was such that the Rovers' fans on the covered terrace taunted him for the rest of the evening, while he tried to spend as much time as possible outside his area.

That proved to be difficult as Rovers were in irresistible form and Taylor wrapped up his hat trick on 56 minutes to become the first player since Rickie Lambert to score two hat tricks in a season for The Gas.

1 Matty Taylor celebrates his second hat trick of the season
2 Tom Lockyer heads clear under pressure from Billy Paynter
3 Lee Mansell shields the ball from Lee James
4 It was a comfortable night for Steve Mildenhall
5 Chris Lines gets away from Jake Gray
6 Rory Gaffney celebrates scoring the second goal of the night
7 Three young Gasheads enjoying the game

■ ■ ■ **Meadow Lane – Saturday 5th March 2016** ■ ■ ■

Notts County **0-2** Bristol Rovers

Referee: Mark Haywood
Attendance: 5,052

Goals: Montano (44), Brown (50)

Almost five years after their last visit to Meadow Lane, when they won 1-0 courtesy of a Will Hoskins goal, Rovers returned to the banks of the River Trent looking for their ninth away win of the current campaign.

Stuart Campbell and Craig Hinton had been tasked with the job of keeping Rovers in League One back then and, as we all know, they failed by the narrowest of margins.

This time around they were looking for points for a far different reason – to keep them in the hunt for promotion to the very same league they dropped out of five years ago.

They were to find a Notts County side in complete disarray. Supporters had hurled insults at The Chairman and his wife when they played a home game against Dagenham & Redbridge four days earlier and for him that was the final straw. One day later he put the club up for sale and, with the Chief Executive having resigned as well, County were a rudderless ship.

The fans weren't happy, either, with manager Jamie Fullarton, the former Rovers Youth Team Manager. Although he had only recently been appointed, they were calling for his head.

Once the game began he spent the entire ninety minutes on the edge of his technical area, seemingly oblivious, but obviously aware, of the malicious abuse being hurled at him.

Rovers boss Darrell Clarke had made just one change to his starting lineup, recalling Jermaine Easter for the injured Rory Gaffney while Ryan Broom and Rory Fallon returned to the bench.

Clarke's plans took a blow with the game

Notts County: *Loach, Atkinson, Hewitt, Audel, Adams (Sharpe, 90), Campbell (Burke, 79), Thompson, Milsom, Banton, Mcleod (Murray, 72) Stead* **Substitutes:** *Carroll, Smith, Hollis, Noble*

Bristol Rovers: *Mildenhall, Clarke (J), Lockyer, McChrystal, Brown, Bodin, Mansell, Lines, (Clarke (O), 86), Lawrence (Montano, 3), Easter (Fallon, 88) Taylor* **Substitutes:** *Leadbitter, Parkes, Puddy, Broom*

only a minute old as Liam Lawrence went down and stayed down after suffering what was later diagnosed as a calf injury. He limped off and was replaced by Cristian Montano who almost scored with his first touch. His shot was parried away by Scott Loach and although Easter closed in to slot home the rebound, he lost his footing at a crucial moment and the chance was gone.

Montano did score in the 44th minute, though, slotting home after a delightful pass from Matty Taylor to register his first Rovers goal.

Five minutes after the restart Lee Brown rifled home his fourth goal of the season following a short corner routine and it was game over.

I've never seen such a one sided second half as Rovers totally dominated proceedings and could have won by four or five.

The football was outstanding and although there were no further goals, Easter, Taylor, Chris Lines and Lee Mansell all went close in a match that was enjoyed by 1,108 Gasheads who had made the trek to the East Midlands.

1 Rovers fans watched the action from the comfort of the Jimmy Sirrel Stand

2 Cristian Montano fires Rovers into the lead

3 Come on you Blues!

4 Tom Lockyer shields the ball from Izale McLeod, watched by skipper Mark McChrystal

5 As the weather worsens, Matty Taylor goes down under a challenge from Adam Campbell

6 Jermaine Easter, under pressure from Curtis Thompson

7 Lee Brown, scorer of Rovers second goal, outpaces Graham Burke

■ ■ ■ **The Memorial Stadium – Tuesday 8th March 2016** ■ ■ ■

Bristol Rovers **3-1** AFC Wimbledon

Goals: Easter (29), Clarke (O) (38), Taylor (78)

Referee: Ben Toner
Attendance: 7,778

Goal: Meades (52)

Inevitably this time of the year is referred to as the business end of the season, and I guess it's totally appropriate given that teams have so many games to play in such a short space of time.

This game was an added extra as the original fixture, scheduled for Saturday 6th February, had been called off due to the Memorial Stadium pitch being waterlogged.

These two sides were, therefore, playing their third game in a week and maybe that was why it was such an open and entertaining spectacle, though more on that later.

The Dons had been in fine form since then and now occupied the final play off spot.

Manager Darrell Clarke had brought in another player on loan on the day of the game, clinching the signature of Swansea City's Scottish U-19 international Oliver McBurnie on loan until the end of the season.

The new signing had to be content with a place on the bench on this occasion, though there were hopes that he might repeat what he did on his debut for Newport County and score a hat trick

after going on as a second half substitute.

The manager made three changes to his starting lineup, even though his side had won their previous two games. Tom Parkes, Ollie Clarke and Daniel Leadbitter returned in place of Mark McChrystal, Billy Bodin and Liam Lawrence.

For the second successive game central defender Tom Lockyer was facing one of his former bosses. The previous Saturday it had been ex Rovers Youth Team Coach

Bristol Rovers: *Mildenhall, Leadbitter (Montano, 90), Clarke (J), Parkes, Lockyer, Brown, Mansell (McChrystal, 85), Clarke (O), Lines, Easter (McBurnie, 59), Taylor*
Substitutes: Harrison, Broom, Puddy, Fallon

AFC Wimbledon: *Roos, Fuller, Robinson, Sweeney, Meades, Smith (Barcham, 36), Bulman, Reeves, Rigg, Taylor (Akinfenwa, 80), Elliott (Azeez, 36)*
Substitutes: Shea, Kennedy, Fitzpatrick, Gallagher

Jamie Fullarton, while on this occasion his former Cardiff City Academy Manager Neal Ardley who is now the AFC Wimbledon gaffer.

It took 29 minutes for Rovers to take the lead in this encounter when Jermaine Easter headed past goalkeeper Kelle Roos. Ollie Clarke doubled the advantage with 38 minutes on the clock when delivering one of his trademark piledrivers.

Jon Meades reduced the deficit seven minutes after the break and there were numerous chances for both sides to score before Matty Taylor, with his 19th goal of the season, settled the game in favour of The Gas who had goalkeeper Steve Mildenhall to thank for preserving their lead when it was only 2-1.

The visitors ended the match with ten men after Adebayo Akinfenwa was red carded for what appeared to be verbal abuse directed at the referee after a free kick had been given against him. He had been on the pitch for all of ten minutes!

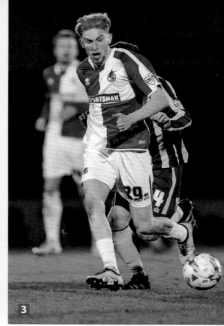

1 Ollie Clarke celebrates his goal, helped by Daniel Leadbitter

2 Matty Taylor goes for goal

3 Oli McBurnie, pictured on his Rovers debut

4 Jermaine Easter heads home the opening goal

5 A determined header by Tom Lockyer

6 Lee Brown gets to the ball ahead of Dannie Bulman

7 At least one person smiled for the camera!

Bristol Rovers **1-0** Mansfield Town

Goals: Taylor (61)

Referee: Dean Whitestone
Attendance: 7,847

Although Rovers had played, and beaten, Mansfield earlier this season, the home fixture against The Stags was of great and significant importance to Bristol Rovers supporters.

It was them, after all, who banged the final nail in our coffin less than two years ago when a goal by Colin Daniel condemned Rovers to fifth tier football for the first time in their history.

With hindsight, of course, it proved to be a good thing and enabled manager Darrell Clarke to rebuild a club and drag it back up, by its bootlaces, into the Football League and turn them into serious promotion challengers in their first season back.

Rovers could also boast three connections with their visitors. Manager Darrell Clarke is a former Mansfield player as is midfielder Liam Lawrence, while defender Tom Parkes was born a stone's throw from the East Midlands town.

Inevitably, in the build up to the game Clarke was asked about his memories of the day that saw his side fall through the trapdoor to The Conference and he always gave the same response, saying that it had been the worst day of his life

and that the pain of that day still hurt him even now.

He's matured as a manager since that time and for this game he sent out a side looking to win a fourth consecutive game for the second time this season, with three changes to the side that beat AFC Wimbledon just a few days earlier.

Cristian Montano, Mark McChrystal and Billy Bodin came in for Ollie Clarke, Tom Parkes and Daniel Leadbitter. And

Bristol Rovers: *Mildenhall, Clarke (J), Lockyer, McChrystal, Brown, Bodin, Mansell, Lines (Clarke, (O) 83), Montano, Easter (McBurnie, 62), Taylor (Harrison, 87)*
Substitutes: Leadbitter, Parkes, Puddy, Broom

Mansfield Town: *Shearer, Alfei, Tafazolli, Collins, Pearce, Benning, Lambe (Beardsley, 64), Clements, Rose (Thomas, 88), Blair (Daniel, 53), Green*
Substitutes: Chapman, Jensen, McGuire, Baxendale

the side reverted to a 4-4-2 formation.

Mansfield's intent was pretty obvious from the off; they had a point and, having lost their last three games, they intended to leave with one.

Neither goalkeeper had a serious save of note to make during a fairly turgid first half though things did liven up a little bit after the break.

The game was just over an hour old when Matty Taylor, lurking at the far post, pounced on a volleyed cross from Montano and struck his 20th goal of the season. In doing so he became the first Rovers striker to register his 20th goal in successive seasons since Jamie Cureton in 1998/99 and 1999/2000.

One goal was enough, though not for the first time this season Rovers had to be grateful to Steve Mildenhall who made an astonishing save from a Lee Collins header in the closing stages to preserve his side's lead.

It was a fitting finale to Clarke's 100th game in charge and sweet revenge for the final day defeat almost two seasons before at the hands of the same opponents.

1 Celebrating Matty Taylor's goal
2 Oli McBurnie on the ball
3 Lee Mansell attempts to dispossess Chris Clements
4 Cristian Montano evades a tackle

5 Steve Mildenhall saves from Lee Collins
6 Jermaine Easter is closely watched by Ryan Tafazoli
7 Full and partial face paint!

Newport County **1-4** Bristol Rovers

Goal: Rodman (3)

Referee: Graham Salisbury
Attendance: 3,663

Goals: Clarke (O) (15), Montano (55), Taylor (61), Harrison (85)

Rovers travelled to Newport looking for revenge for the 4-1 defeat inflicted on them by the Welsh club last October and seeking a fifth consecutive victory.

Rodney Parade, where The Exiles now play, is shared with rugby union side Newport Dragons and that was obvious as soon as we arrived for this 12.30pm kick off.

Remember when rugby and football were both played at The Mem and the pitch would have very little grass on it at this time of the year? Well, you can imagine just how the playing surface looked for this match. Depending on who you spoke to, between 15 and 30 tons of sand had been dumped, literally, on the pitch in an attempt to make it playable following recent heavy rain in the Principality - and then rolled in. As a result, the playing surface resembled Weston beach after the tide goes out.

The teamsheets, when they arrived in the press area, showed one change to the Rovers starting lineup with Rory Gaffney, back from injury, replacing Jermaine Easter.

By then I had received a phone call asking me to make sure that Ryan Broom reported

to the dressing room immediately, which indicated there was a problem as he had already done his own warm up and was the player left out of the party of 19 that made the short trip over the Severn Bridge.

It turned out that Lee Mansell had sustained a calf injury in the warm up and his place in the starting lineup went to Ollie Clarke, with Broom taking his place on the bench.

Newport County: *Day, Holmes (O'Sullivan, 65), Jones (Davies, 87), Donacien, Hughes, Rodman, Ayina, Byrne, Elito, Wilkinson (Klukowski, 75), Boden*
Substitutes: Barrow, Green, Morgan, Partridge

Bristol Rovers: *Mildenhall, Clarke, Lockyer, McChrystal, Brown, Bodin, Lines, Clarke (O), Montano, (Broom,85), Gaffney, (McBurnie, 58), Taylor (Harrison, 75)*
Substitutes: Leadbitter, Parkes, Easter, Puddy

Rovers made the worst possible start to the game as the home side scored after just three minutes when Alex Rodman collected a misplaced Gaffney pass on the halfway line and waltzed through the Rovers defence before firing a shot past Steve Mildenhall from the edge of the area that went in off the post.

The response was swift and came from Ollie Clarke after just 15 minutes when he rifled an unstoppable equaliser past home custodian Joe Day.

All square at the break, and a fairly even contest, I think most of us thought it would be more of the same after the break, but Rovers had other ideas and were completely dominant, scoring three more goals to register an emphatic win.

Cristian Montano's left foot volley gave Darrell Clarke's side the lead, Matty Taylor's 20th league goal of the campaign and 21st overall, made it 3-1 and Ellis Harrison, Newport born and bred, added goal number four when he intercepted a horrendous back pass by Janoi Donacien and rolled the ball past Day.

Oh, and to cap an eventful afternoon, Broom got to make his league debut!

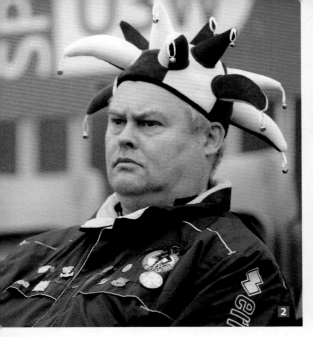

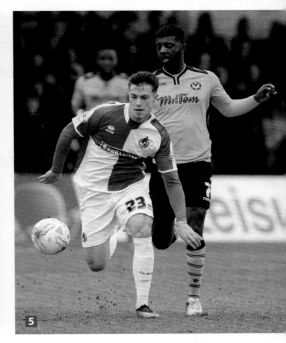

1 Ryan Broom is about to make his Rovers league debut

2 Hats on for this one!

3 Oli McBurnie takes on Ben Davies

4 Cristian Montano beats Alex Rodman to the ball

5 Billy Bodin on the ball

6 A determined run by Ollie Clarke

7 Two of Rovers goalscorers, Matty Taylor and Cristian Montano, celebrate

■ ■ ■ The Memorial Stadium – Friday 25th March 2016 ■ ■ ■

Bristol Rovers 3-0 Cambridge United

Goals: Bodin (10 & 18), Taylor (73)

Referee: Stephen Martin
Attendance: 10,262

Rovers headed into this game looking for a sixth consecutive victory and a fifth league double of the season, safe in the knowledge that they would be watched by one of the biggest crowds at The Memorial Stadium this season.

For one Rovers player, namely Rory Gaffney, the game was one to look forward to following his move to The Memorial Stadium from Cambridge earlier this year and after a successful loan spell prior to that.

He was named in a starting lineup that saw manager Darrell Clarke make just one change and that saw Daniel Leadbitter return in place of Tom Lockyer, who was away on international duty with the Welsh U-21 squad.

Lockyer was one of three Rovers players missing through international commitments; Ellis Harrison was also with Wales while on loan Swansea striker Oli McBurnie was with the Scottish U-21 squad.

With three players on international duty, you would expect a club to be able to call off their league game, but a ridiculous ruling prevents this from happening when one of the players is signed on an emergency loan, as McBurnie was, so Rovers had no choice but to play the game.

Bearing in mind that they were also missing the injured Lee Mansell and Stuart Sinclair, the fact that they went on to record an emphatic victory speaks volumes about this squad.

The biggest attendance of the campaign did turn up - the 10,262 being 72 more than the gate for the match against Plymouth Argyle in January.

There were a few early scares for Clarke's side and goalkeeper Steve Mildenhall made two fine saves in the opening two minutes.

However, once Billy Bodin had opened the scoring on 10 minutes there were few anxious moments for the home supporters. Bodin's strike was a little fortunate in that it was a long range effort that seemed to catch visiting goalkeeper Will Norris off guard, though that didn't matter to the home fans; their side were ahead and it was going to stay that way.

Eight minutes later Bodin added a second goal when his glancing header from Leadbitter's cross went in off the bar. Incredibly, in a career that has taken in almost 150 games, it was the first time he had scored twice in a first team match.

The visitors almost pulled a goal back on 66 minutes, but Mildenhall made an outstanding close range save from Josh Coulson before Matty Taylor scored his 22nd goal of the season with 73 minutes on the clock, to cement his club's place in the top three.

Bristol Rovers: Mildenhall, Leadbitter, Clarke (J), McChrystal, Brown, Bodin, Lines, Clarke (O (Lawrence, 71), Montano (Parkes, 75), Gaffney (Easter, 79), Taylor
Substitutes: Puddy, Broom, Malpas, Fallon,

Cambridge United: Norris, Furlong, Coulson, Legge, Haynes, Ismail (Roberts, 71), Berry (Clark, 55), Dunne, Dunk, Spencer (Simpson, 55), Williamson
Substitutes: Beasant, Horne

1 Billy Bodin, who scored twice in a league game for the first time in his career

2 An aerial battle between Mark McChrystal and Leon Legge

3 Matty Taylor on the ball

4 A high challenge on Ollie Clarke by Luke Berry

5 Jermaine Easter is challenged by Ryan Haynes

6 Rory Gaffney beats Leon Legge to the ball

7 Face painting was the order of the day!

■ ■ ■ **Brunton Park – Monday 28th March 2016** ■ ■ ■

Carlisle United **3-2** Bristol Rovers

Goals: Stacey (11), Wyke (59), Kennedy (85)

Referee: Darren England
Attendance: 4,718

Goals: Bodin (28), Taylor (57)

A light training session at the Memorial Stadium the morning after the victory over Cambridge, was all there was time for before the long trek up to Carlisle for this Easter Monday fixture.

The team left at 8.00am on Easter Sunday and, after a break for refreshments at a motorway service station, arrived at the team hotel at 2.00pm.

Travelling the short distance to the ground on the morning of the game, with kit manager Marco Carota, we weren't sure what to expect as Brunton Park had been hit badly by this winter's floods, so much so that Carlisle had played home games at Blackpool, Preston and Burnley as their pitch had been several feet under water.

The playing surface had been relaid, and looked in surprisingly good condition when we arrived.

Behind the scene though, it was obvious that there was still a great deal of work to do to return offices and the boardroom back to their former glory.

Most of the staff were working out of three portakabins in the car park, and would continue to do so, we were told, until the summer. Still, everyone was

friendly in spite of what they had been through, especially one of the stewards who told us that he and his wife had been rescued from their house at the height of the floods by firemen using an upturned fridge as a boat!

As for the game it was one that got away from Darrell Clarke's side, in a match where both sides were poor, defensively.

The manager made one change to his starting XI, drafting in new father Tom Parkes at the expense of Daniel Leadbitter.

Carlisle United: Gillespie, Miller, Ellis, Raynes, Gillesphey, Stacey (Joyce, 62), Comley, Kennedy, Grainger (Ibehre, 66), Gillead (Pedro, 73), Wyke
Substitutes: Atninson, Smith, Hanford, Asamoah

Bristol Rovers: Mildenhall, Clarke (J), Parkes, McChrystal, Brown, Bodin, Lines, Clarke (O) (Lawrence (22), Montano (Easter, 22), Gaffney (Leadbitter, 82), Taylor
Substitutes: Puddy, Broom, Malpas, Fallon

However, his side fell behind with 11 minutes on the clock, Jack Stacey's long range effort going in off the post.

Billy Bodin equalised on 28 minutes, stabbing the ball past a hesitant defender and goalkeeper after running on to Jermaine Easter's ball into the box.

Easter and Liam Lawrence had entered the fray after 22 minutes, as the manager was far from happy with what he was seeing.

Carlisle scored again, through Charlie Wyke, five minutes into the second half but once Matty Taylor had got his side back on level terms for the second time, Rovers grabbed the game by the scruff of the neck and tore into their opponents.

As so often happens, though, when a team is so much on top, they are hit by a sucker punch and that's what happened here with five minutes to go, Jason Kennedy taking advantage of some slack marking to blast a shot past Steve Mildenhall to give Carlisle all three points.

1 Brunton Park ready for action!

2 Cristian Montano takes on Jason Kennedy

3 Happy before kick off!

4 James Clarke gets past Danny Grainge

5 Matty Taylor rues a missed opportunity

6 Chris Lines on the ball

7 Billy Bodin celebrates his goal

■ ■ ■ **The Memorial Stadium – Saturday 2nd April 2016** ■ ■ ■

Bristol Rovers **3-0** Crawley Town

Goals: Taylor (54 & 78), Lawrence (75)

Referee: Fred Graham
Attendance: 8,250

Having ended March with a defeat after six consecutive wins, Rovers were determined to get back to winning ways as they returned to The Memorial Stadium to take on Crawley Town.

In spite of the defeat at Brunton Park, which had seen his side slip down to fifth place in the league standings, manager Darrell Clarke and his squad appeared relaxed in the build up to what many supporters were billing as a must win game.

The manager, who had been highly critical of his side's defending against Carlisle made three changes to his starting lineup that saw Daniel Leadbitter, Tom Lockyer and Liam Lawrence return in place of James Clarke, Tom Parkes and Cristian Montano.

Lockyer was returning from international duty, as were substitutes Ellis Harrison and Oli McBurnie.

The three had met with mixed fortunes as 'Locks' and Ellis had been in the Welsh U-21 side that drew one and lost one of their European qualifying matches. To make things worse, Ellis had missed a penalty in the defeat. McBurnie on the other hand, had scored his first Scottish U-21 goal.

Whilst it was expected a crowd in excess of 9,000 would turn up for the match, the club had to settle for 8,250, only 99 of whom had travelled to support the visitors.

The Crawley manager, Mark Yates, was no stranger to The Mem, having been here on a number of occasions with his previous employer, Cheltenham Town, and he included three former Rovers players in his starting lineup.

Matt Harrold had enjoyed mixed fortunes

Bristol Rovers: *Mildenhall, Leadbitter, Lockyer, McChrystal, Brown, Bodin, Lines, Clarke (O), Lawrence (Montano, 77), Gaffney (McBurnie, 83), Taylor (Easter (84)*
Substitutes: Parkes, Harrison, Clarke (J), Puddy.

Crawley Town: *Preston, Young, Yorwerth, Bradley, Dunne, Edwards, Bond, Sutherland (Walton, 76), Della-Verde, Harrold (Barnard, 84), Deacon (Fenelon, 64)*
Substitutes: Rose, McNerney, Ashton, Bawling

in a Rovers shirt, but was always a player who gave 100%, though in his time at The Mem he spent too much time in the treatment room.

Andy Bond and Lyle Della-Verde played only a handful of games for The Gas in their respective loan spells and many people didn't even recognise their names on the teamsheet!

The opening 45 minutes of this game showed why so few had made the trek down to Bristol to watch Crawley. Their sole aim appeared to be to prevent Rovers from scoring and in that they succeeded.

Whereas the Rovers side of old might also have accepted a point, Clarke's squad are made of sterner stuff and once Matty Taylor had headed in from a Liam Lawrence corner there was only going to be one winner.

Lawrence added a second, with a sublime free kick, on 75 minutes and the irrepressible Taylor added a third three minutes later, heading home from another corner, this time Chris Lines providing the delivery.

The goals took Taylor's goal tally to 25 for the season and the points moved Rovers back up to third.

1 Matty Taylor's header beats goalkeeper Callum Preston to put Rovers 1-0 ahead

2 Lee Brown brings the ball under control, watched by Gwion Edwards

3 C'mon the Gas!

4 Liam Lawrence beats Josh Yorwerth to the ball

5 Billy Bodin takes on Frankie Sutherland

6 Tom Lockyer clears his lines, watched by former Rovers striker Matt Harrold

7 Chris Lines eases past former Rovers midfielder Lyle Della-Verde

■ ■ ■ **Sixfields Stadium – Saturday 9th April 2016** ■ ■ ■

Northampton Town **2-2** Bristol Rovers

Goals: Adams (23), Hoskins (29)

Referee: Tony Harrington
Attendance: 7,579

Goals: Taylor (76), Harrison (88)

Sixfields doesn't hold very special memories for me, as every time I go there I am reminded of a night back in May 1998 when The Cobblers beat Ian Holloway's side in a play-off semi-final.

Rovers had established a 3-1 lead in the first leg but they were bullied by a physical home side, managed by Ian Atkins, and were beaten 3-0.

Having almost gone out of business earlier in the season and with staff and players going without pay for a number of weeks, the story of Northampton's season is quite remarkable as victory against Rovers could well see them crowned champions with five games to go.

There had been changes to the dressing room area since our last visit with it now being double the size of the previous facility. Opposite the players' tunnel is a half completed stand that will, eventually, increase the stadium's capacity.

For this game manager Darrell Clarke had the luxury of naming an unchanged side following the win against Crawley Town. There was, though, a change on the bench where Jake Gosling came into

the squad for the first time since 28th December, and following a loan spell with Newport, in place of tonsillitis victim Oli McBurnie.

The player who isn't the most popular amongst Rovers supporters, John Joe O'Toole was in the Northampton lineup. O'Toole scored the only goal of the game when the clubs met on the opening day of the season and he wasn't the only player in the home squad with Rovers connections.

Northampton Town: *Smith, Moloney, McDonald, Diamond, Buchanan, Holmes, Rose, O'Toole, Adams (D'Ath, 76), Marquis (Taylor, 82), Hoskins (Collins, 76)*
Substitutes: Byrom, Potter, Prosser, Clarke

Bristol Rovers: *Mildenhall, Leadbitter, Lockyer, McChrystal, Brown, Bodin (Easter, 71), Clarke (O), Lines, Lawrence (Montano, 56), Gaffney (Harrison, 56), Taylor*
Substitutes: Parkes, Clarke (J), Gosling, Puddy

Goalkeeper Ryan Clarke, who might have returned to The Mem last summer, expressed his regret that he made the wrong choice as he has warmed Northampton bench all of season.

As for the match, Rovers bossed the opening 20 minutes and a cross from Bodin grazed the crossbar early on.

However they gifted the home side an opening goal, gratefully accepted by Nicky Adams, and found themselves two goals down on 49 minutes when another gift wrapped opportunity was accepted by Sam Hoskins.

Matty Taylor's sublime back flick, from Daniel Leadbitter's cross, saw Rovers pull a goal back with 14 minutes to go and Ellis Harrison, making his 100th league appearance for the club, netted a dramatic equaliser two minutes from time to earn a point that could be crucial come the end of the season.

The result was enough for the home side to have their promotion to League One confirmed, while 925 Rovers fans at the match and another 1,100 watching on the big screen at The Mem were satisfied with their team's point.

1 A different view of Sixfields Stadium

2 Billy Bodin closes in on Rod McDonald

3 Happy Gas fans!

4 Ellis Harrison is about to begin the celebrations after his late equaliser

5 Matty Taylor celebrates his goal

6 Chris Lines gets the better of John Marquis

7 Goalscorers Ellis Harrison and Matty Taylor in a relaxed mood before the game

Bristol Rovers **2-1** Yeovil Town

Goals: Gaffney (42), Taylor (77)

Referee: Andrew Madley
Attendance: 10,264

Goal: Lita (73)

Rovers' first win of the current campaign came at Yeovil in their second league game of the season when Ellis Harrison's late goal secured all three points.

Since then, of course, Rovers have gone on to mount a strong challenge for automatic promotion and another victory over their Somerset rivals might well put them in a top three place.

However The Glovers arrived at The Mem in a buoyant mood for, having flirted with the bottom two places in the league before Christmas, they had managed to lift themselves clear of trouble.

Much of the credit for that goes to manager Darren Way who, since taking over from Paul Sturrock, had managed to stop the rot and his side came into this game seeking the three points that would ensure League 2 survival.

Way, of course, has served his club well for a number of years as a player, coach and now manager. Since taking over as boss at Huish Park he has made his side very difficult to beat. They arrived at The Memorial Stadium a week after suffering their first home defeat since he took over.

A number of players have turned out for both clubs in recent times, including Gavin Williams, JP Kalala and our own Marcus Stewart. However none of the players on view for this game had the distinction of playing for both outfits. There was, though, one player in the Yeovil Town squad with Bristol connections and Leroy Lita's spell at Ashton Gate meant that he would be taunted mercilessly by Gasheads in the bumper crowd of 10,264.

Bristol Rovers: Mildenhall, Leadbitter, Lockyer, McChrystal, Brown, Bodin, Clarke (O), Lines, Montano (Easter, 76), Gaffney (McBurnie, 88), Taylor (Harrison, 80)
Substitutes: Parkes, Mansell, Lawrence, Puddy

Yeovil Town: Krysiak, Roberts, Sokolik, Smith, Dickson, Walsh, Shephard, Dolan (Laird, 77), Goodship (Lita, 58), Compton (Bird, 58), Zoko
Substitutes: Tozer, Weale, Campbell, Lacey

Darrell Clarke made just one change to his starting lineup, recalling Cristian Montano at the expense of Liam Lawrence and his side asked all of the first half questions against a stubborn Yeovil outfit.

Clarke's side dominated possession but all they had to show for their first half exertions was a 42nd minute goal from Rory Gaffney, who headed past Artur Krysiak from Billy Bodin's free kick.

The second half proved to be quite an open affair and the aforementioned Lita livened up proceedings on his arrival with 58 minutes on the clock.

He equalised with an angled drive across Steve Mildenhall and was then booked for his over exhuberant celebrations which involved taking his shirt off (why do players do that when they know the consequences?).

Rovers, though, had the last laugh as Matty Taylor scored his 27th goal of the season just four minutes later.

Rovers did survive a few anxious moments, though, as Mildenhall made a point blank save from Ryan Baird and Marc Laird somehow managed to hit the crossbar when a goal looked inevitable.

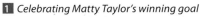

1 Celebrating Matty Taylor's winning goal

2 Polska Gas wait for kick off

3 Rory Gaffney hurdles over Ryan Dickson

4 Billy Bodin is determined to get to the ball first

5 Matty Taylor munches his way through another shirt!

6 Daniel Leadbitter keeps a close watch on Brandon Goodship

7 Stuart Sinclair received the Sky Bet League 2 Unsung Hero award for March prior to kick off

■ ■ ■ **The Lamex Stadium – Tuesday 19th April 2016** ■ ■ ■

Stevenage **0-0** Bristol Rovers

Referee: Andrew Madley
Attendance: 3,836

When the two sides met at The Memorial Stadium last November, Teddy Sheringham had been in charge and saw his side win by two goals to one.

Sheringham, though, didn't last too much longer in his first venture into management and became just another statistic when he joined the ranks of sacked bosses this season.

And so it was caretaker manager Darren Sarll who prepared his side for this game knowing that one point would secure League 2 football at The Lamex Stadium for another season.

The only previous occasion Rovers had visited Stevenage was, as previously mentioned, back in August 1998 when they were known as Stevenage Borough and the then non-league outfit's stadium was plain old Broadhall Way!.

The stadium has changed a lot in the intervening years, but is far too red for my liking. Still, it's a friendly club boasting a stand, used for visiting supporters, behind one goal and another all seater stand running the length of the pitch underneath which are the dressing rooms and club offices. The remaining two sides of the ground consists of covered terracing.

Rovers boss Darrell Clarke, who had seen his side move up to third place in the league standings following victory against Yeovil, made three changes to his starting lineup for this match. In came Jake Gosling, James Clarke and Tom Parkes and out went Billy Bodin, Cristian Montano and Mark McChrystal. In fact the skipper was left out of the squad altogether.

Gosling was back in the side for the first time since Boxing Day last year and

Stevenage: Jones, Henry, Wilkinson, Wells, Franks, Mulraney (Lee, 90), Tonge, Parrett, Pett, Luer (Kennedy, 72), O'Connor
Substitutes: Keane, Day, Okimo, Conlon, Gorman

Bristol Rovers: Mildenhall, Leadbitter (Bodin, 46), Clarke (J), Lockyer, Parkes, Brown, Clarke (O), Lines, Gosling (Easter, 71), Gaffney (Harrison, 59), Taylor
Substitutes: Mansell, Puddy, Montano, McBurnie

following a loan spell with Newport County. It was he who went close to breaking the deadlock when his sweetly struck half volley grazed the Stevenage post in the 21st minute.

That came in the middle of a purple patch for Rovers, who had soaked up some early pressure from a home side keen to secure a win to confirm their Football league status.

For all their possession, though, they seldom threatened Steve Mildenhall's goal and were happy to take their time at set pieces.

As the half drew to a close Daniel Leadbitter fired wide when well placed. It was his last taste of the action as he didn't reappear for the second half when Clarke decided to change formation.

Neither side could make that all important breakthrough, though, with goalscoring opportunities at a premium. The closest Rovers came to scoring came from a Billy Bodin effort that was touched round the post by Jamie Jones.

Scrappy it might have been, but the point gained could well prove to be crucial come the end of the season.

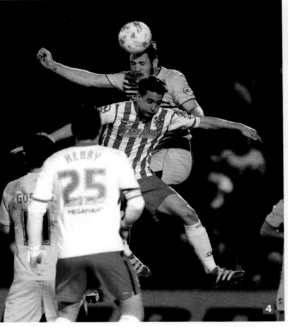

1 Rovers supporters behind the goal that Rovers defended in the first half

2 Tom Lockyer beats Aaron O'Connor to the ball

3 Jake Gosling on the ball

4 Tom Parkes wins this header

5 Jermaine Easter tussles with Dean Parrett

6 Ollie Clarke beats Dean Parrett to the ball

7 Tense on the touchline

■ ■ ■ The Memorial Stadium – Saturday 23rd April 2016 ■ ■ ■

Bristol Rovers **3-1** Exeter City

Goals: Bodin (13), Brown (45), Taylor (69)

Referee: Nigel Miller
Attendance: 10,254

Goal: Brown (48)

Just a week after one West Country side had visited The Memorial Stadium, another came visiting, this time in the shape of Exeter City, still in with an outside chance of making a play off place in spite of a midweek defeat at the hands of Mansfield Town.

Unusually for such a local game, there was only one player who had connections with both clubs and that was Jordan Tillson. The son of former Gas legend, Andy, had spent his formative football years with Rovers but was released without being offered a contract. Now a squad member with The Grecians, he was named on the bench for this game.

Rovers boss Darrell Clarke labelled this game as the biggest test for his side since last season's Wembley play off final against Grimsby Town and once again a home crowd in excess of 10,000 arrived at The Mem expecting nothing less than three points (that is, apart from the 893 Exeter fans included in that total!)

Clarke made four changes to his starting lineup, recalling Mark McChrystal, Lee Mansell, Billy Bodin and Cristian Montano in place of Tom Parkes, Ollie Clarke, Jake

Gosling and James Clarke and his side took the game to their opponents from the off.

Montano and Bodin had both gone close before the former set up the latter to open the scoring on 13 minutes, when he lashed a left foot shot past goalkeeper Bobby Olejnik.

Although Exeter enjoyed spells of possession in the opening 45 minutes, Steve Mildenhall was seldom troubled

 Bristol Rovers: Mildenhall, Leadbitter, Lockyer, McChrystal, Brown, Bodin, Mansell (Lawrence, 90), Lines, Montano (Clarke (O), 62), Gaffney, Taylor (Easter, 84)
Substitutes: Parkes, Harrison, Puddy, Easter

Exeter City: Olejnik, Ribeiro, Brown (Nicholls, 61), Moore-Taylor, Woodman (McAllister, 54), Holmes (Grant, 86), Noble, Harley, Taylor, Watkins, Stockley
Substitutes: Davies, Reid, Pym, Tillson

and his side doubled their lead on the stroke of half time thanks to a moment of indiscipline by central defender Troy Brown.

Having tangled with Matty Taylor on the edge of the area he needlessly shoved the Rovers striker to the ground after the ball had been cleared and was booked for his indiscretion. His namesake, Lee, punished him and his team mates even more as he rifled the resulting free kick into the corner of the net.

Three minutes after the break Exeter pulled a goal back when Jake Taylor's curling shot beat Mildenhall and the goal signalled some anxious moments, from those watching as well as the players out on the pitch, as the visitors went in search of an equaliser.

However Matty Taylor's 69th minute goal, his 28th of the seasom, restored the two goal advantage and gave Clarke's side some breathing space.

David Noble did have a shot blocked before the end and substitute Joel Grant saw two more shots blocked by a packed Rovers defence before the final whistle but Rovers held out to maintain their quest for an automatic promotion spot.

1 A celebration with a difference from Billy Bodin!
2 Cristian Montano takes on Christian Ribeiro
3 The only way is up!
4 Lee Brown gets in a cross

5 Rory Gaffney is challenged by Jordan Moore-Taylor
6 Matty Taylor goes for goal
7 Chris Lines gets a shots away

York City **1-4** Bristol Rovers

Goal: McEvoy (81)

Referee: Darren Handley
Attendance: 4,525

Goals: Bodin (19 & 71), Easter (80), Mansell (88)

Bootham Crescent was the venue for the final away game of the season and Rovers travelled to Yorkshire still intent on equalling the number of away wins (11) in a season.

Hotel prices in York had almost doubled for this Bank Holiday weekend which would see the Tour of Yorkshire cycle race pass through the city, so Darrell Clarke and his side stayed in Leeds the night before the match, some 35 minutes away.

York's relegation to The National League had already been confirmed, though they had defeated play off hopefuls Portsmouth on home territory two weeks before this match.

Nothing less than a win would do for Clarke's side, who went into the match in fourth position and hoping that Accrington and Oxford would slip up and that victory would see them back in an automatic promotion place.

There would be no lack of support for his side, as a travelling Gas army numbering 2,000 had bought tickets to see their team in action and another 900 or so would be watching the game on the TV screens back at The Memorial Stadium.

Bootham Crescent hasn't changed much over the years and the majority of the Rovers fans found themselves watching from an open terrace behind one goal, while around 200 were seated in the end wing of the adjoining stand that ran the length of the pitch and also housed a number of home supporters.

The covered home terrace was sparsely populated by a small number of home supporters and the main stand, an old wooden construction, housed more home supporters and a cramped press box.

York City: *Flinders, Hendrie, Winfield, Bennett, Cameron, Berrett, Penn (Carson, 59), Summerfield, Galbraith (McEvoy, 59), Fewster, Alessandra*
Substitutes: Riordan, Swan, Thompson, Dixon, Ingham

Bristol Rovers: *Mildenhall, Leadbitter, Lockyer, McChrystal, Brown, Bodin, Mansell, Lines, Montano (Gosling, 65), Gaffney (Harrison, 78), Taylor (Easter, 78)*
Substitutes: Parks, Clarke (O), Puddy, McBurnie,

Clarke named an unchanged side for the match, while on the bench Jake Gosling came in for the injured Liam Lawrence. Following some early pressure his side took the lead when Billy Bodin fired a left foot shot past Scott Flinders to register his 11th goal of the season.

There were no further goals until Bodin added his, and Rovers, second on 72 minutes, and two quickly became three as substitutes Gosling and Jermaine Easter combined for the latter to beat Flinders from close range.

The home side responded immediately and pulled a goal back through Kenny McEvoy.

Rovers weren't finished and scored again when Gosling's shot was blocked and the rebound fell to Lee Mansell who rifled a shot past the unfortunate Flinders.

News that both Accrington and Oxford had also won tempered the post-match celebrations, leaving the fate of all three clubs to be decided on the final day of the season.

1. The view from the away end as the teams come out on to the pitch
2. Mark McChrystal battles for possession with Bradley Fewster
3. Daniel Leadbitter's challenge sends Danny Galbraith to ground
4. Billy Bodin is about to score his second goal of the game
5. Cristian Montano on the ball as Luke Hendrie closes in
6. Jermaine Easter celebrates his goal
7. Now it's time for Lee Mansell to celebrate!
8. A family day out at York

■ ■ ■ The Memorial Stadium – Saturday 7th May 2016 ■ ■ ■

Bristol Rovers 2-1 Dagenham & Redbridge

Goals: Bodin (15), Brown (90)

Referee: Stuart Atwell
Attendance: 11,130

Goal: Cash (12)

The last Saturday of the season and for the third year running Bristol Rovers had a home fixture with something riding on it.

Two years ago they needed to beat Mansfield Town, but lost 1-0 and ended their 94 year stay in the Football League.

Last season a 7-0 thrashing of Alfreton Town wasn't good enough to pip Barnet to The Vanarama Conference and they had to gain promotion the hard way, through the play offs.

This time around they needed to beat already relegated Dagenham & Redbridge and hope that one of the two clubs immediately above them, Oxford and Accrington Stanley, dropped points.

A win would put them on 85 points and that total is usually good enough to cement an automatic promotion spot – would that be the case this year?

Darrell Clarke's side had already equalled a club record for the number of away wins in a season (11) and now, as well as bidding for automatic promotion, they were looking for a ninth consecutive home win for the first time since 1983/84, while victory would also mean a 13th win from the last 14 (the other game having been drawn).

No one really pointed it out beforehand, but it was also the manager's 100th league game in charge. Eight of those were in the ill-fated relegation season two years ago, 46 in The Vanarama Conference and another 46 in League Two this season.

No one was thinking of records, though. All the talk was about securing automatic promotion rather than having to do it via another trip to Wembley. Surely Wycombe would deny their local rivals, Oxford,

Bristol Rovers: Mildenhall, Leadbitter, Lockyer, McChrystal, Brown, Bodin, Mansell (Easter, 80), Lines, Montano (Gosling, 55), Gaffney (Harrison, 66), Taylor
Substitutes: Parkes, Clarke (O), Puddy, McBurnie

Dagenham & Redbridge: Cousins, Shepherd, Hyam, Dikamona (Connors, 46), Pennell, Chambers (Cureton, 74), Raymond, Boucaud (Hawkins, 87), Hemmings, Cash, Doidge
Substitutes: McClure, Hyde, Heather, Moore

victory, and just as surely Stevenage would prove to be party poopers at Accrington... wouldn't they?

In all honesty I think supporters were more nervous than players. Before a ball had been kicked in anger last August, many I spoke to would have accepted finishing mid table after the shock of experiencing one season of non-league football.

Clarke and his squad, though, had other ideas and targeted a top seven finish at the very least. The manager has built a squad confident in their own ability and they are a very relaxed group who have, in my opinion, never shown signs of any pressure getting to them.

A great many pundits had labelled them as over achievers, given their lofty league position and the fact that it is a squad full of free transfers and players who are coming to the end of their first season in league football.

Personally I think that's an insult to a very honest and talented group of players who have worn the shirt with pride this season and who have restored everyone's faith in this unique club. People have said the same about Leicester City, and no doubt they have said it about the three clubs

standing above Rovers before this game, namely champions Northampton and the aforementioned Oxford and Accrington.

As for team selection, Clarke named an unchanged starting lineup and bench for this crucial fixture whilst his opposite number John Still, a former Rovers assistant manager, elected to leave former Rovers striker Jamie Cureton on the bench.

There were early chances for Rovers, Billy Bodin seeing a shot parried away by goalkeeper Mark Cousins, and Matty Taylor glancing a header wide from Lee Brown's corner. It wasn't all one way traffic, though, as The Daggers looked good in possession and quick on the counter attack and they caught Rovers out with 12 minutes on the clock.

Matty Cash took advantage of the time and space afforded to him to rifle a low shot past Steve Mildenhall and the noise generated by a crowd in excess of 11,000 was silenced.

The good news was that Oxford and Accrington had failed to score in their games and, in any case, Rovers were behind for only three minutes.

Bodin, at his brilliant best, slalomed around three challenges inside the area before slotting a shot past Cousins for the equaliser, and the noise that greeted the goal was deafening.

However, the goal avalanche expected by supporters after that never materialised and although there were chances to build up a decent half time lead, they weren't taken.

Rory Gaffney headed wide when well placed, Tom Lockyer glanced a header wide following a corner, Gaffney was denied by a superb save from Cousins and Mark McChrystal headed over from all of two yards.

There were anxious moments at the other end, it must be said, as Dagenham looked anything but a side that will be playing football in The National League next season. Steve Mildenhall made decent saves from Matty Cash, Andre Boucaud and Ashley Chambers, while Frankie Raymond hit a free kick over the crossbar.

There were no further goals, though, and we reached half time all square as did the games involving our two rivals for automatic promotion.

That scenario changed nine minutes into

the second half when Oxford went ahead against Wycombe. Rovers, though, were struggling to score a second and Taylor hit a shot wide after news of the Oxford goal while Jake Gosling and Chris Lines both saw efforts blocked before Taylor's deflected shot hit the bar and dropped behind for a corner.

News of a second Oxford goal filtered through on 72 minutes, so it was almost certain that a second and, hopefully, winning goal was required at The Mem… just as long as Accrington didn't decide to get their shooting boots on!

Taylor saw two more efforts saved by the inspired Cousins, and there was a dangerous moment at the other end but Tom Lockyer cleared off the line from Christian Doidge.

Jermaine Easter, McChrystal and Taylor again went close but as the clock ticked towards the 90 minute mark, it looked as though the play offs were beckoning.

Supporters sat near the press box couldn't bear to look and buried their heads in their hands – something I've only ever seen before in penalty shootouts, not during normal time!

As the board went up showing extra time we heard that Oxford had scored a third goal and they had secured promotion.

Accrington, though, were still playing

and still goalless. Two minutes into the four added on, Taylor created another chance for himself but, agonisingly, his effort struck the post and rebounded into play. Cue 11,000 groans that quickly became something else as the marauding Lee Brown popped up to slot home the rebound with his right foot.

How fitting that a player who has featured in every minute of every game this season, and who chose to stay with the club following relegation two years ago, should score such an important goal on the day that his partner, who was in the crowd, was due to give birth to their second child.

I digress; never have groans turned to cheers more quickly and once again manager Clarke showed his sprinting prowess, moving at a rate of knots from dugout to corner flag to celebrate with his players who were piled on top of one another in front of the covered terrace formerly known as the Blackthorn End.

Noise levels were on the crescendo scale and 'Irene' has never sounded so good. The final two minutes seemed to take an age as Rovers slowed things down knowing there was a possibility they had done enough.

At the final whistle supporters poured on to the pitch, but the drama wasn't over. They seemed to have forgotten that Accrington were still playing and as

we desperately waited for news to come through the Radio Bristol headphones it was carnage out on the pitch; there wasn't a blade of grass to be seen.

And then came the news we all hoped for. Accrington had played out a goalless draw with Stevenage and Rovers had leapfrogged them in the league table to clinch third spot on goal difference.

Everyone went mental, the decibels rose again and The Gas were definitely going up. League One Football beckons, two years after the drop into The Conference. History had been made as the manager everyone has taken to their hearts achieved what no other Rovers boss has ever done; back to back promotions.

We later discovered just how close it had been as Accrington had hit the bar in the final minute of their match, after the Rovers game had ended. It mattered not though, as the celebrations were well under way and Gasheads can now look forward to awaydays against Bolton Wanderers, Sheffield United and Coventry, as well as renewing acquaintances with local rivals Swindon Town.

It's been an incredible journey over two years and who is to say that the journey can't continue under new owners who must think the job is a doddle having witnessed just two defeats in their 16 game tenure.

3 *Lee Brown is under there somewhere!*
4 *Here's to a Rovers win!*
5 *Matty Taylor heads for goal*
6 *Chris Lines takes on Frankie Raymond*
7 *Billy Bodin has just equalised*
8 *Mark McChrystal rises to the occasion!*
9 *Rory Gaffney in the thick of the action*

■ TWO TO ONE ■

sky BET LEAGUE 2

PROMOTED 2016
BRISTOL ROVERS

WE'RE GOING UP!

Acknowledgements

The support that Bristol Rovers achieved in the 2015/16 season was truly remarkable and those who attended games, home and away, really were the twelfth man in another successful season that saw the club achieve back to back promotions for the first time in their history.

This record of the 2015/16 season is dedicated not only to them but to Gasheads in this country and all over the world who, in spite of being unable to attend matches, still show their support for this unique football club. During the course of the season I receive numerous messages from Gasheads who live overseas, all of whom tune in to listen to commentary on our games and for many that means keeping very unsociable hours!

A quick glance at social media sites also shows the level of support for the club, which is both welcome and appreciated.

While the events of two years ago will never be forgotten, the way that everyone has continued to show their support for this club makes me, as always, proud to be a Gashead.

In addition to the credits detailed below, I would like to place on record my thanks to club historians Stephen Byrne and Mike Jay who willingly gave up their free time to proof read this publication, along with Business Development Manager Karim Mardam-Bey.

Credits

Written by Keith Brookman

Design and production by Ann Walter

Photography by JMPUK, in particular Joe Meredith, Neil Brookman, Rogan Thomson, Dougie Allward, Alex James and Robbie Stephenson

Edited by Stephen Byrne and Mike Jay

Printed by Pensord, Blackwood, South Wales

Published by Tangent Books

The following players were allocated squad numbers for the 2015/16 season

1	Steve Mildenhall
2	Daniel Leadbitter
3	Lee Brown
4	Tom Lockyer
5	Mark McChrystal
6	Tom Parkes
7	Lee Mansell
8	Ollie Clarke
9	Ellis Harrison
10	Matty Taylor
11	Jake Gosling
14	Chris Lines
15	James Clarke
16	Nathan Blissett
16	Liam Lawrence
17	Jermaine Easter
18	Dominic Thomas
19	Danny Greenslade
20	Jamie Lucas
21	Cristian Montano
22	Kieran Preston
23	Billy Bodin
24	Stuart Sinclair
25	Will Puddy
26	Tyler Lyttle
27	Ryan Broom
28	Jay Malpas
29	Jeffrey Monakana
29	Paris Cowan-Hall
29	Oliver McBurnie
30	Aaron Chapman
30	Rory Gaffney
31	Lee Nicholls
32	Alfie Kilgour
33	Rory Fallon